GOLF

Steps to Success

Second Edition

DeDe Owens, EdD
Teaching Professional
Cog Hill Golf & Country Club, Lemont, Illinois

Linda K. Bunker, PhD
Professor, Curry School of Education
University of Virginia, Charlottesville

Human Kinetics

Library of Congress Cataloging-in-Publication Data

Owens, DeDe.
   Golf : steps to success / DeDe Owens, Linda K. Bunker. -- 2nd ed.
      p. cm. -- (Steps to success activity series)
   ISBN 0-87322-578-3 (pbk.)
      1. Golf. I. Bunker, Linda K. II. Title. III. Series.
   GV965.087 1995
   796.352'3--dc20   95-1518
                                                                  CIP

ISBN: 0-87322-578-3

Developmental Editor: Judy Patterson Wright, PhD; **Assistant Editor:** John Wentworth; **Proofreader:** Sue Fetters; **Typesetter and Layout Artist:** Denise Lowry; **Text Designer and Illustrator:** Keith Blomberg; **Cover Designer:** Jack Davis; **Photographer (cover):** Wilmer Zehr; **Printer:** United Graphics

Instructional Designer for the Steps to Success Activity Series: Joan N. Vickers, EdD, University of Calgary, Calgary, Alberta, Canada

Human Kinetics books are available at special discounts for bulk purchase. Special editions or book excerpts can also be created to specification. For details, contact the Special Sales Manager at Human Kinetics.

Printed in the United States of America   10 9 8 7

Human Kinetics
Web site: www.humankinetics.com

United States: Human Kinetics, P.O. Box 5076, Champaign, IL 61825-5076
800-747-4457
e-mail: humank@hkusa.com

Canada: Human Kinetics, 475 Devonshire Road, Unit 100, Windsor, ON N8Y 2L5
800-465-7301 (in Canada only)
e-mail: orders@hkcanada.com

Europe: Human Kinetics, Units C2/C3 Wira Business Park, West Park Ring Road
Leeds LS16 6EB, United Kingdom
+44 (0) 113 278 1708
e-mail: hk@hkeurope.com

Australia: Human Kinetics, 57A Price Avenue, Lower Mitcham, South Australia 5062
08 8277 1555
e-mail: liahka@senet.com.au

New Zealand: Human Kinetics, P.O. Box 105-231, Auckland Central
09-523-3462
e-mail: hkp@ihug.co.nz

CONTENTS

PREFACE

Understanding the game of golf is a lifelong challenge. The book *Golf: Steps to Success* is the compilation of our experiences over 50 years of golf and gives us an opportunity to share what we have learned about this wonderful game. The contents of this book represent not only our own past experience and research but also the collective knowledge of LPGA and PGA professionals who have freely shared information from their experiences.

Playing the game of golf requires active participation throughout learning. Within each step (chapter) of this book you will find information about the specific skills required to be successful in golf and strategies for learning these skills.

This book differs from other golf books in that it provides clear guidelines for practice and immediate recording of your progress. It is designed for *active* learning. The sections on "Success Stoppers" identify typical problems experienced by golfers and provide specific suggestions for correcting those problems. These suggestions can often be applied either on the practice tee or during a round of golf.

This new edition includes over 80 drills and practice techniques to help you improve your skills. The illustrations are clear and show you exactly what to do to lower your scores. Both mental and physical skills are incorporated so that you can use all of your resources to improve your game. We suggest ways to set your own pace and adjust challenges. The content of this edition has been reorganized to provide you every opportunity to evaluate your own skills. In addition, there is a new section on etiquette that would make any golf course or country club proud to have you play there.

Taking this book with you when you practice as a handy reference for drills and to review technique will allow you to gain immediate feedback by comparing your performance to the desired goals. Each activity is designed to provide a motivating opportunity for practicing golf and to help you become a self-learner.

You will never be too good to quit learning about the game of golf. After you master the steps in this book, you may wish to progress to *Advanced Golf: Steps to Success*. From the beginner to professional, most golfers are students of the game all their lives. Half the fun is learning how to hit a draw or hook when you *want* to—not when it happens to you accidentally. You can learn to challenge a course in the same way that you accept challenges and opportunities in other aspects of your life, for golf is a lifetime sport.

Just as others have helped us, we hope these *Steps to Success* will help you become a motivated student of golf. We would particularly like to acknowledge the Jemsek family, owners of Cog Hill Golf Course in Lemont, Illinois, and Wilson Sporting Goods for the opportunity to constantly test and reevaluate teaching strategies and drills that challenge golfers and allow us to refine our teaching philosophy. Like most knowledge, ours has come from many sources, including fellow golf professionals and educators. Though it would be impossible to acknowledge each one individually, we would like to thank them collectively for the years of sharing ideas about the game of golf and the challenges of teaching it.

THE STEPS TO SUCCESS STAIRCASE

G et ready to climb a staircase to golf success. Just like any staircase, it is not possible to leap to the top. You get there by climbing one step at a time. Each of the 12 steps you will take has been planned in sequence as a natural progression from the one before. The first few steps of the staircase provide a foundation—a solid base of skills and concepts. As you progress further, you will be able to execute the basic golf swing and modify it to meet any situation on the course. You will learn to choose the proper clubs and swing to match your various golf preferences and needs—whether for loft, trajectory, or distance. As you near the top of the staircase, the climb eases, and you will find that you have developed a sense of confidence in your golf ability that makes further progress a real joy. After you have mastered these steps, you may wish to progress to *Advanced Golf: Steps to Success*.

Familiarize yourself with the first sections of this book, including the information on Equipment and The Game of Golf, for an orientation and to understand how to set up your practice sessions around the steps.

Follow the same sequence each step (chapter) as you climb the staircase to golf success.

1. Read the explanations of what is covered in the step, why the step is important, and how to execute or perform the step's focus, which may be a basic skill, concept, tactic, or combination of all three.

2. Follow the numbered illustrations showing exactly how to position your body to execute each basic skill successfully. There are three general parts to each skill: preparation (getting into the right position), execution (performing the skill that is the focus of the step), and follow-through (ending position after ball is struck). These are your keys to success.

3. Study the Success Stoppers that list common errors along with the recommendations on how to avoid or correct them.

4. Practice the drills to help you improve your skills through repetition and purposeful practice. Read the directions and Success Goals for each drill. Then review the Success Checks and practice accordingly. Be sure to record your score and compare your performance with the Success Goals for each drill. Because the drills are arranged in an easy-to-difficult progression, you need to meet the Success Goals of each drill before moving on to practice the next one. This sequence is designed specifically to help you be a self-learner who is continually progressing as a golfer. Pace yourself by adjusting the drills to either increase or decrease difficulty, depending on where you are.

5. As soon as you can reach all the Success Goals for one step, you're ready for an impartial observer to evaluate your basic skill technique against the Keys to Success found at the beginning of each step. The observer should be an experienced golfer or pro who can help you assess your technique and form. This is an important addition to the information you receive from watching the resulting ball flight for each shot.

6. Repeat these procedures for each of the 12 Steps to Success. Then rate yourself according to the directions for "Rating Your Golf Progress." Using this form and the Shotkeeper Scorecard (see appendix), you can continue to improve your golf game, increase your level of enjoyment, and lower your handicap by carefully tracking your on-course play.

Good luck on your step-by-step journey of developing your golf skills, building confidence, experiencing continuous progress, and having fun on your way to golf success.

THE GAME OF GOLF

The exact origin of golf is unknown. Some historians believe the earliest form of golf may have emerged in Greece, where ancient shepherds hit stones with their staffs. However, the game as we know it today had its origins in St. Andrews, Scotland, around 1744. In 1888 the first officially recorded golf club was established in Yonkers, New York, by three Scotsmen. This first course had six holes scattered through cow pastures and an apple grove and was named in honor of their Scottish homeland course, St. Andrews. Today a regulation course has 18 holes and may cover as many as 250 acres of beautifully groomed countryside. Golf is enjoyed today as a popular recreational activity. It can lead to various levels of competition. Golf is also a growing spectator sport, with professional and amateur tournaments becoming very popular.

Playing the Game

The object of the game of golf is to hit a small, hard ball — the *golf ball* — as few times as is necessary for it to travel from its starting point, on the *tee*, into the *hole* located on each green. The golf ball is struck with clubs designated as *woods* or *irons*. Each player must hit his or her own stationary ball in the desired direction and for the desired distance, using one of a variety of clubs of assorted lengths and shapes. Each attempt to strike the ball, whether successful or unsuccessful, is called a *stroke*.

You may play a game of golf alone or in a group with one to three other players. Golf is played on golf courses with 9 or 18 holes. The holes vary in length from 85 to 600 yards and are generally referred to as short holes (85-245 yards), medium holes (245-445 yards), or long holes (445-600 yards). The total yardage of a regulation 18-hole golf course varies from 5,600 to 7,200 yards.

In addition to the lengths of the holes, golf courses have other characteristics that provide challenges to players (see Figure 1). Each hole begins from a teeing area (tee box) from which the first ball must be hit. Each hole ends on a *green*, which has a 4 1/4-inch diameter hole, or *cup*, cut down into the grass on the green. Between the tee and the green is the *fairway*. The course is designed with specific boundaries that are marked by out-of-bounds stakes. A player who hits a ball outside the boundary or into water is penalized by having one stroke added to the score.

All golf holes have the five components described: teeing area, fairway, rough, putting green, and cup (hole). The central path from tee to green is the fairway, and it is the preferred location for your ball's landing. These areas may be wide or narrow, smooth or rough, and may have trees and shrubs located within them. Unfortunately, sometimes shots land in the taller grass left alongside the fairway, called the *rough*, which may also have natural obstacles such as trees and wooded areas. The ball may also land in sand or water hazards. Such challenges on the golf course are called *hazards* or *trouble*.

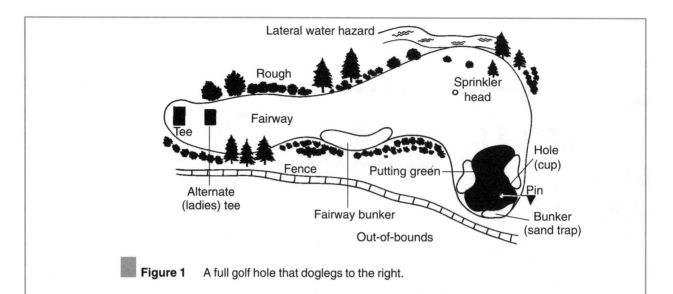

Figure 1 A full golf hole that doglegs to the right.

Scoring

Your ability as a golfer is measured by the number of strokes it takes you to complete each hole. The count begins with the first attempt to hit the ball off the tee. One stroke is counted each time you attempt to hit the ball (whether it is contacted or not) until it goes into the cup on the green of that hole. Your score for a round of golf is the total number of strokes for the 9 or 18 holes played. Lower scores are indicative of better players and are normally reported as the total of 18 holes, which is called a *round*.

It is possible to compete against another golfer and win by using fewer strokes to complete the round. Otherwise, you may wish to measure your ability against a designated standard of excellence called *par*. Par is the number of strokes judged to be necessary for a very good golfer to complete a hole. It is assumed that a golfer requires two putts once the ball has landed on the green. If you add to the putts (two) the number of shots it should take to reach the green, you can determine par. The number of strokes is determined by the length of the hole: par 3s are short holes (85-245 yards), requiring only one stroke from tee to green and two putts; par 4s are medium-length holes (245-455 yards); and par 5s are long holes (over 455 yards). If you are a very good golfer and you play a 480-yard hold, for example, it should take you three shots to get to the green and two putts, for a par 5. In order to add challenge to the golf course, the lengths of holes are varied. On a typical 18-hole course there are four par 3s, ten par 4s, and four par 5s, for a course par of 72.

There are terms in golf that reflect how you score on a hole relative to par. An *ace* is a hole on which it took only one swing to land in the hole — also known as a *hole-in-one*. This is a very unusual occasion and is cause for great celebration! An *eagle* refers to 2 strokes under par on a hole, whereas a *birdie* is 1 stroke under par. It is common to take more strokes than par; taking 1 stroke more than par is called a *bogey*, whereas 2 strokes over par is referred to as a *double bogey*.

After a round, golfers often talk about their games relative to how they played, not always in relation to their score. And like most other sports, there is a special language and set of terms that describe that play. For example you will hear golfers refer to "fairways hit," "greens in regulation," "sandies," "up and downs," "chip ins," and "number of putts."

Fairways hit refers to the tee shot and where the ball lands as a result of that shot. If the ball ends up in the fairway versus the rough, it is a "fairway hit." Shots from the fairway tend to be easier to hit than from other areas, so it is to your advantage to hit as many fairways as possible.

Greens in regulation refer to the number of strokes it took you to get to the putting surface, in relation to the hole's difficulty. For example, on a par-4 hole, it is assumed that it takes two shots to get to the green, since it is always assumed that it takes 2 putts (4-2=2). This is an ideal standard, and the term refers to how many times you accomplished this ideal standard.

Sandies are shots taken from sand bunkers. Learning to play sand shots is fun. And becoming efficient at hitting them close to the pin can be very rewarding in lowering your score, not to mention your sense of accomplishment. Sandies reflect this proficiency in terms of the number of times you hit from the sand and then sink the following putt.

Up and down refers to the same principle as "sandie," but reflects other shots such as chips and pitches. The idea is to get the ball "up" onto the green, and "down" into the hole with as few strokes as possible.

Number of putts relates to the total number of putts for the round. In general, it is assumed that there will be 2 putts on each hole, and this number is calculated into the course rating. Putting is a skill that everyone can learn quickly and achieve a degree of success at with practice.

Basic Rules

The rules of golf are designed to provide a fair chance for all players to play at their best levels and to compete fairly against one another or against the course (against par). The rules provide the framework for direction and order in the game, so the sooner you understand them, the more fun you will have. If you do not use them as intended, you may find yourself needlessly penalized or accused of cheating.

Golf rules are often described by the nature of the penalties incurred for certain course conditions or behaviors. When a rule is violated, it can result in penalties of 1 or 2 strokes, or disqualification. There are also some conditions on the course over which you have no control and for which you are assessed a penalty.

The official rules of golf contain specifications related to the actions of players preparing to strike the ball, conditions surrounding the ball at rest, and course conditions independent of the player's control. A brief review of the most important rules for stroke play (which is more often used by beginners and social golfers than is match play) and commonly encountered situations are presented in these *Steps to Success*. However, when you are ready to compete, you should purchase an official rule book and read the rules of golf published by the United States Golf Association, Far Hills, NJ 07931.

No Penalty: Free Drop

Shots coming to rest in the conditions listed here are beyond your control and therefore do not result in penalties. If you find yourself in any of these situations, you may hit the ball as it lies. Otherwise, "seek relief" which is a "free drop," which allows you to relocate the ball in the fairest way possible. To drop a ball at the "nearest point of relief" means to stand outside the trouble area, face the hole, extend your arm at shoulder height, and literally drop the ball within two club lengths (see Figure 2). The ball must be dropped within two club lengths to the point of release and come to rest at a spot no nearer the hole than the original spot from which relief is sought.

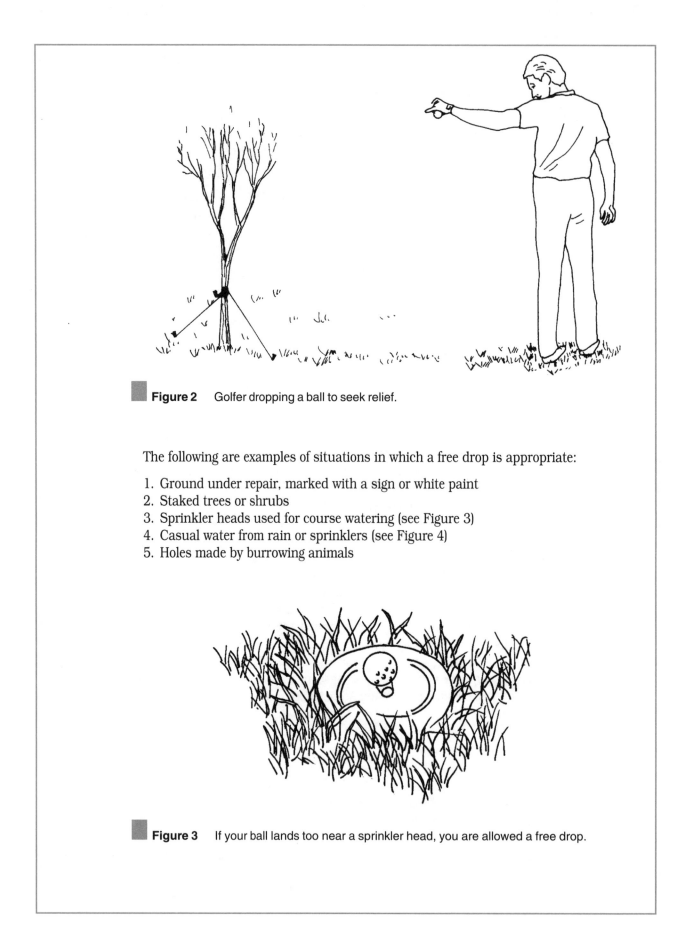

Figure 2   Golfer dropping a ball to seek relief.

The following are examples of situations in which a free drop is appropriate:

1. Ground under repair, marked with a sign or white paint
2. Staked trees or shrubs
3. Sprinkler heads used for course watering (see Figure 3)
4. Casual water from rain or sprinklers (see Figure 4)
5. Holes made by burrowing animals

Figure 3   If your ball lands too near a sprinkler head, you are allowed a free drop.

■ **Figure 4** Casual water from rain or a sprinkler allows you a free drop.

One-Stroke Penalty

Each of the following situations results in a one-stroke penalty. In addition, there are specific procedures required in order to continue. These specifications are provided with each of the following situations.

1. A *lost ball* is one that cannot be found within 5 minutes. "Drop" another ball at the point from which your original ball was hit, or return to the tee if originally hit from the teeing area (see Figure 5).

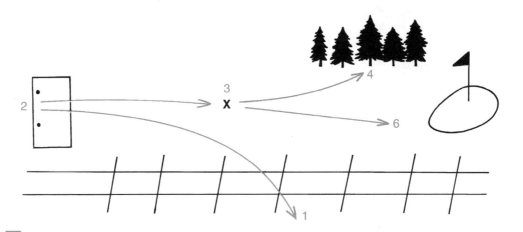

■ **Figure 5** Assume first ball went out-of-bounds. Return to tee and hit (penalty + stroke = 3). Land at X. Hit ball out-of-bounds into woods, return to X and hit (penalty + stroke = 6).

2. An *out-of-bounds* ball is one that has gone beyond the white stakes placed on the perimeter of the golf course. (If any part of the ball lies inbounds, the ball is considered inbounds and in play.) Go back to the spot from which the ball was hit and drop it, or retee

a ball hit from the teeing area. If you think you have hit your ball out of bounds, it is common practice to hit a "provisional ball" before leaving the original location. If you find your first shot inbounds, you must play it and simply pick up your second ball.

3. A *direct water hazard* is water that runs across the fairway, perpendicular to the fairway. It is usually marked by yellow stakes that designate that the hazard consists of all the area within the stakes, which may include marshy ground and other land, as well as water (see Figure 6).

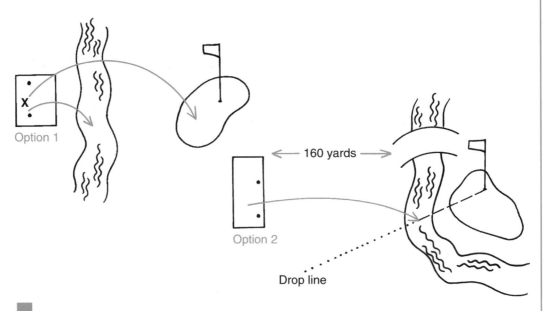

Figure 6   Two direct water hazard examples.

Option 1: Go back to original spot (X) and drop another ball. Or play a provisional ball from the original spot as soon as you see your first ball go into the water.

Option 2: Keeping on line with the point where the ball crossed the margin of the hazard, go back away from the pin as far as desired and drop the ball.

4. A *lateral water hazard* is water that runs parallel to the fairway. It is usually marked with red stakes designating that every point within the area is considered part of the hazard (see Figure 7).

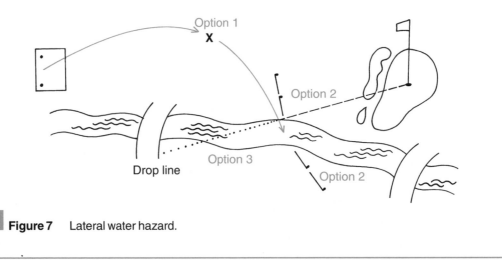

Figure 7   Lateral water hazard.

Option 1: Go back to the shot's original spot and drop another ball.

Option 2: Determine where the ball would have crossed the far margin of the hazard had it gone over it. Drop a ball within 2 club lengths of that spot, but no closer to the hole.

Option 3: Go to the far side of the hazard directly across from where the ball entered the hazard. Drop a ball as far away as desired on the line that could be drawn from the pin through the ball.

5. An *unplayable lie* is any shot you consider unplayable. It can be any ball except one in a water hazard (see Figure 8).

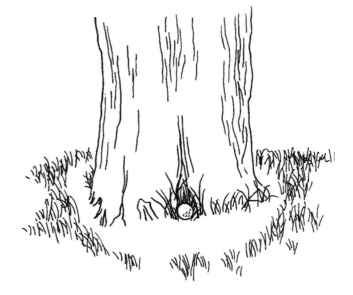

Figure 8   An unplayable lie results in a one-stroke penalty.

Option 1: Go back to original spot and drop another ball.

Option 2: Drop a ball within 2 club lengths of the ball's position, but no closer to the hole.

Option 3: Go back as far as desired to drop the ball on a line from the pin through the unplayable point.

6. An *accidental moving of ball* occurs when a ball moves from its original position because a player accidentally touches it. The ball must be returned to its original position.

7. *Whiffing* happens when you attempt to hit the ball, but no contact is made. This is the same as a strike in baseball. The swing counts as a stroke; leave the ball there and try again!

Two-Stroke Penalty

Each of the following situations results in a 2-stroke penalty, and must be accompanied by the following actions if specified.

1. *Grounding the club in a hazard.* You must not let your club touch the ground while in a hazard, whether preparing to strike the ball or on the backswing. The club may touch the hazard as part of the forwardswing (see Figure 9) or follow-through.

Figure 9   Grounding a club in a hazard (at any time before the actual swing) results in a 2-stroke penalty.

2. *Hitting the wrong ball.* If you discover you have hit the wrong ball, find the correct ball and play it. Count only the strokes taken on the correct ball, but add a 2-stroke penalty.

3. *Hitting a ball or flag on the green.* When putting *from the green*, you must not hit the flag or another golfer's ball with your ball. It is your responsibility to have the "flag tended" and moved aside (see Figure 10). Also, it is up to you to have an opponent "mark" his or her ball if it is in the way of your putt. Play the ball from where it comes to rest. An opponent's ball that has been moved must be replaced to its original position.

4. *Requesting assistance.* In regulation play, only general course knowledge may be requested from others. For example, you may ask for the length of a hole, but it is not legal to ask for advice about what club to use or to request help on your swing.

Disqualification

1. You can be disqualified for hitting the wrong ball and not correcting the error prior to teeing off on the next hole. To avoid this, check the ball each time before you swing to be sure that it is yours.

2. You can be disqualified for making an error in scoring, assigning a lower score than you earned to any hole.

Some of the rules of golf require that you return to the place of an original shot after assessing a penalty. If you have hit a long drive, this can be a problem in that it takes a great deal of time to go down to look for the ball and then walk all the way back to the original spot to hit another ball. For this reason it may be a good idea to hit a *provisional ball.* A provisional ball is a ball played from the same spot as the last shot, when it is feared that the original ball has just landed out-of-bounds or is lost outside a water hazard. If the

■ Figure 10   Hitting a flag from a putt on the green results in a 2-stroke penalty.

original ball is found inbounds, it must be played; the provisional ball must then not be used.

The rules of golf are not always easy to interpret or remember. It is therefore a good idea to carry a rule book in your golf bag. If you are playing in a tournament and are in doubt as to the interpretation of a rule, ask for assistance from a tournament official. It is also sometimes appropriate to agree among playing partners to reinterpret strict rules during the learning stages or if playing conditions are very poor. For example, in early spring some golf courses allow you to improve your ball's lie, due to the large number of bare spots on the course. This is sometimes referred to as playing *winter rules*.

Sometimes rules are so difficult to interpret that there is a question of what to do. In that case, it is possible to play a second or *alternate ball* for the rest of a hole. The player must state which ball will count after a ruling is obtained. If it is not stated prior to playing the two balls, the ball with the higher score must count.

As a player, you are responsible for knowing the rules and playing by them. Unfortunately, not all players know the rules, and/or some choose not to apply them. If you are playing with such a player, consider your options: Inform him or her of the rules, share your rule book, assess the penalty, or ignore him or her and play your own game. In a tournament, you must inform the golfer of the rules. If the infraction is not corrected, assess the penalty. In social golf, the decision is up to you.

Golf Etiquette

There are many unwritten courtesy rules that are an integral part of the game of golf. For example, only one golfer ever hits at any one time. There is no penalty for violating a "rule of etiquette," but such offenses are considered extremely rude and unacceptable. Just like many other sports, there are certain unwritten rules of the game that signal others that you really know what is going on. Course etiquette and the social rules of the game of golf are very important.

Golf is often referred to as a game for gentlemen (and gentlewomen). When you play golf, you are expected to be courteous and to play by the rules. You are expected to make rule interpretations and call stroke penalties on yourself. You are also expected to treat your playing partners and the course with respect.

Good golfers not only play honestly, but they respect their opponents and respect the game. For example, if you hit a shot into the woods, you must either find it or take a penalty; if the ball moves out of position when you address it, you must add a penalty stroke to your score. You are your own official. In contrast, how often have you seen a team sport player admitting to an umpire or referee that he or she accidentally stepped out-of-bounds or committed a foul?

The rules of golf are carefully set down by the United States Golf Association (USGA) and the Royal and Ancient Golf Club of St. Andrews (R & A, the organization that governs golf in Great Britain). These rules are not intended to limit your play or enjoyment, but rather to guarantee it by selecting the rules that are the fairest to all players and to the integrity of the game.

In addition to the official rules, there are also unofficial rules of etiquette that are designed to maximize the enjoyment of golf for everyone. The following tips to good golf etiquette summarize several courtesies that are generally expected on the golf course.

Ten Keys to Successful Golf Etiquette

There are ten areas in which you are expected to demonstrate appropriate social behavior. These include playing in groups, teeing off, understanding the order of play, behavior on greens, playing without delay, safety, course care, use of carts, appropriate dress, and being courteous to fellow golfers.

1. Playing in Groups

The game of golf is generally played with two to four persons in a group. It is, of course, possible to play by yourself, but generally people play in groups of up to four golfers. Because golf has become such a popular game, some golf courses require that you play in foursomes in order to make the course available to the greatest number of golfers. At such courses, you may be asked to play with other golfers of differing abilities. Fortunately, the handicapping system helps to make it fun to play with persons of many different abilities. Also, knowing the acceptable rules of etiquette helps your enjoyment when playing with new friends.

2. Teeing Off

When you want to play a round of golf, you are generally assigned a tee time. This is the time you and your partners are scheduled to hit your first ball and begin playing the round. If you are playing a course for the first time you may want to call to find out whether you need to reserve a specific tee time or whether you will be given a tee time upon arrival at the course. This means arriving at the course with enough time to spare so that you can warm up, hit some balls from the practice tee or putt some on the practice green, and still be ready to tee off at the designated time. If you are not there on time, you might not be allowed to play at all.

Tee Off on Time

1. Make reservation for tee time.
2. Warm up ahead of time. Do your warm-up routine (stretching), hit balls on practice tee, practice on putting green.
3. Tee off on time (first person hits at designated time).

The first person to hit on the tee is said to "have the honors." On the first hole, the honors are determined by a flip of the coin. In social golf or a foursome, the first tee honors are not formally determined. General practice suggests that the most senior golfer, women, or the lowest handicap tees off first. For each hole after that, honors are given to the person with the lowest score on the previous hole. If two people scored the same, the honors remain with the person who had them on the previous hole, or if neither of the tied golfers had the last honors, their previous order of hitting remains in effect.

3. Order of Play on Fairway

Once all golfers have teed off, the golfer with the farthest distance yet to go to the green plays the next shot. All other golfers should wait behind an imaginary line through this golfer's ball so that safe golf can continue (see Figure 11). Once the golfer has hit the ball, all golfers walk on toward their own balls or to the green, but they do not pass another golfer who is waiting to hit.

Order of Play on Fairway

1. Golfer farthest away from hole hits first.
2. All others stay behind hitter.
3. Everyone walks on toward own ball.

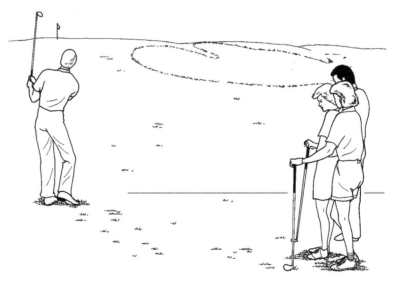

Figure 11 Golfers wait behind imaginary line for safe golf.

4. Behavior on the Green

On the green there are several points of etiquette that are important. You should be aware of the order of putting, the rules and courtesy associated with the flag, and the importance of moving off the green quickly when you have finished putting. Once all players are on the putting green, the player who is farthest away from the hole putts first (this is referred to as being *away*, and is the same general type of rule as on the fairway). If some golfers are near the green but not yet on it, you may give them the option of playing on to the green. There is no rule that says they "must" hit. Some players prefer to hit, others to wait (see Figure 12). For example, if your ball is on the green and 25 feet from the pin, and another player is 10 feet away but in the bunker, give him or her the option to hit onto the green or to wait.

Order of Play on Green

1. All on green first.
2. Longest putt next.

Figure 12   Player farthest from the hole putts first.

If you are on the green and one of your playing partners has a long putt, it is a courtesy to *tend the flag*. By standing with one hand on the flag, you can see the hole clearly and can remove the flag as soon as the ball is stroked (putted) to avoid a possible penalty (if a putted ball hits an unattended flag, there is a 2-stroke penalty). Remember, if the ball is not on the green, it is all right to leave the flag in the hole. You should therefore always ask your partners whether they wish you to "tend the flag" (see Figure 13). If you pull the flag, gently lay it down on the green or the fringe clearly out of the way of any stray putts.

Tending Flag

1. Pull flag to putt if on green.
2. Ask partner to tend flag.
3. Lay flag out of way.
4. If ball is on fringe, leave flag in hole.
5. Never step in the line of another person's putt.

Putting greens are generally well groomed and watered often. Because of this careful care, they may be relatively soft. When you walk on a green, you may leave subtle foot-

Figure 13   Flag tenders use an extended arm to avoid stepping in the line of the putt.

prints. It is therefore important never to take a step in the line of another person's putt. That is, if you can see the line someone's ball will roll along toward the hole; do not step on or near this line.

5. Playing Without Delay

Nothing is more irritating to other golfers than slow players. This does not mean that you must rush your shots, but please make an effort to play with deliberate speed. Always be ready to hit when your turn comes. Walk quickly between shots so that you can take your time over the ball. If you are waiting for another player to hit, be thinking about your shot, select your club, and be prepared to swing. Once it is your turn, use your routine, get set, and swing smoothly.

You should do as much preparation before your turn as is possible. Just be careful not to distract your playing partners. Take your time in selecting the shot, but try to do it before it is literally your turn. Walk quickly between shots so that you have more time during your turn.

Once you and your playing partners have completed a hole, leave the green quickly and walk to the next tee. Then record your score and comment about your putts or chat momentarily if you wish. Never stay on the green and talk, or you may delay the group behind you when they should be hitting their approach shots.

Playing through. If a single golfer or group of golfers behind you is catching up to you and is having to wait continuously before playing their shots, you should let the faster group *play through* if there is room in front of you. Playing through means that the players behind you pass you during the course of play. Allowing others to play through is a very important courtesy on the golf course. For example, if your ball goes out-of-bounds and you have to take time to search for it, check to see whether another group should be "waved through." Once you have signaled this group, be sure that you and your partners stay to the side of the course so that the others can safely play through.

Rapid Play

1. Watch behind you.
2. Walk quickly between shots.
3. Leave green quickly.
4. Record scores on next tee.

Others Playing Through

1. Check before hitting.
2. Allow rapid players to go ahead.
3. Signal approaching golfers when it is safe to hit.

6. Always Be Aware of Safety

Golf is generally considered to be a very safe sport. However, it is played with two potentially dangerous "weapons": the club and the ball. A golf ball can be a deadly weapon if it strikes someone. One of the most vivid examples of the power of the clubbed ball is often demonstrated by "trick shot artists" who can set a piece of 1-inch thick plywood in front of a teed-up ball. When a good drive is executed, the ball goes through the piece of plywood!

Never hit a golf ball until you have checked to see that you have plenty of room to swing your club safely and that the other players on the course are well out of range. If ever in doubt, wait to hit. If you happen to hit a ball toward another golfer, yell *"fore!"* as loud as you can. This is a universal warning signal for golfers and should result in the other golfers ducking or taking cover. Also, when letting a group play through, be sure to watch them hit, so you know where their balls are going.

Safety Tips

1. Check for clearance to swing.
2. Be sure no one is within range of your shot.
3. Hit only when safe.
4. Yell *"fore!"* if your ball may be dangerous to others.

7. Take Care of the Golf Course

The golf course is your playing field. You would not mistreat a hardwood basketball floor or wear your spikes on a clay tennis court—nor should you mistreat the golf course. For example, never drive or pull a golf cart onto a green or tee box. Similarly, be careful where and how you set down a flag if you pull it from the hole.

Replace all divots. When you hit the fairway and take a "divot," or clump of grass, with your swing, stop to replace it. Pick up the divot, return it to the bare spot, and gently step on it (see Figure 14). (In some climates divots may not regrow, so golfers sprinkle sand into the bare spot.) Remember, you would not like to land in such a bare spot, so fix divots for the next golfer.

Rake all bunkers. When you hit from a sand bunker, be sure to rake it smooth before you leave it (see Figure 15). Because you will need to rake it, it is usually smarter to enter the bunker from the shortest distance to the ball. When raking it, walk backward out of the bunker so that you can rake your footprints smooth as you leave the bunker. After you are finished with the rake, place the rake in a safe area with the spikes facing down.

Repair ball marks. Sometimes your ball leaves an indentation when it lands on the green from a great height or distance. If everyone left such marks on the green, it would look dimpled like a golf ball. You should repair these ball marks by inserting a tee or specially designed ball mark repair tool (shaped like a 2-pronged fork) under the depression at an angle and pressing down on it so that its tip elevates the turf to a normal level (see Figure 16). Then gently tap down on the former depression with your putter. If you repair all your ball marks and even others you come upon, the greens will be much smoother and easier to putt for everyone.

Replace Divots

1. Pick up divot (grass).
2. Replace in bare spot.
3. Step on grass.

 Figure 14   Replace all divots and gently stamp down with your foot.

Rake All Bunkers

1. Rake bunker smooth.
2. Walk backward to leave no footprints.
3. Store rake safely.

Figure 15   Raking bunkers leaves them smooth for other golfers.

Repair Ball Marks

1. Identify ball mark.
2. Insert tee under dent.
3. Press down on large end of tee to raise earth.
4. Tap the spot level.

Figure 16   Use a tee to repair ball marks.

8. Use of Carts

Many golfers prefer to wheel their golf bags on carts or to utilize motorized riding carts. Such carts are optional conveniences for golfers and should be carefully located so as not to hurt the grass of the golf course. For example, never wheel or drive a cart onto a green, close to a hazard, or between a green-side bunker and the green. When approaching the green, walk or ride around the green to the side near the next tee; park your cart there. Then, after you have putted, you can replace your putter in the bag and be ready to go briskly to the next tee.

Some golf courses have specific paths for motorized carts. It is essential that you follow these paths and, if the rules of the course require it, stay on the path at all times. If in doubt, always ask. If you are sharing a cart with another golfer, drive it to a location near the position from which you or your partner should hit the next shot or closest to the next tee. Park the cart and either stay with it or walk a short distance to your shot. Then drive on together. It is a courtesy and a rule at some courses to keep the cars 30 feet from the tees and greens.

9. Dress for Success

Many golf courses require appropriate clothing. In general, slacks, golf skirts, or midthigh shorts are appropriate, but some courses do not allow short-shorts or running shorts. Some courses also require collared shirts and do not permit T-shirts or tank tops. The best rule of thumb is to dress conservatively and neatly.

You must wear golf shoes or smooth-soled shoes (like tennis shoes) in order to protect the golf course. It is never appropriate to wear street shoes or shoes with heavy treads or heels.

10. Treat All Players With Courtesy

When playing golf, it is courteous to be quiet and not move while others are hitting or putting. By not disturbing other players, you help them play their best, and they will help you, too.

When someone is about to strike a golf ball, be sure that you are not in his or her line of sight. This generally means staying to the side or behind so that you cannot be seen even in his or her peripheral vision. You must also be careful not to allow your shadow to cross the path of another's putt (see Figure 17). This is a more subtle distracter, but being aware of it is a very powerful indicator to others that you really are a true golfer.

 Figure 17   Do not allow your shadow to cross the path of another's putt.

If you treat all players with courtesy and fairness, they will treat you with the same respect. Remember, it is only fun to play the game when everyone plays under the same conditions. Treat others the way you would like to be treated.

Handicaps

Golf is truly a lifetime sport for people of all ages and abilities. The handicapping system makes golf an ideal sport in which players of differing abilities can compare their performances or compete against each other. Your golf *handicap* is an equalizer so that you can adjust your score. The USGA has a system that calculates handicaps in relation to the difficulty of the course. This *slope system* assigns a rating to each course, which is used to modify your handicap for courses of varying difficulties. To determine your actual handicap, keep track of your scores on 10 rounds of golf and consult your local golf pro. (For a *rough* estimate of your handicap, subtract the course rating (e.g., 72.4) from your average score for 10 rounds (e.g., 100 - 72 = a handicap of 28).

When you're ready to test your skills in competition you will find many opportunities. Public golf courses often sponsor tournaments for players of all levels. In some tournaments the score that counts is your *gross score*, or the total of all the strokes you take. In other tournaments you are allowed to subtract your handicap from your gross score for a *net score*. However, in open tournaments, where professionals and amateurs all can participate, your gross score is the only one used.

There are several organizations that provide clinics and lessons for golfers. Most public and private golf clubs have golf professionals who belong to either the Ladies Professional Golf Association (LPGA) or the Professional Golfers' Association (PGA, with both men and women professionals). Be sure to look for a qualified professional; check with others who have taken lessons with this pro before you invest in a series of lessons.

If you wish to read more about the game or need additional information, contact the National Golf Foundation (NGF). This is a nonprofit organization that provides clinics for teachers, assistance to golf courses, and educational materials on the game of golf. There are also school golf programs sponsored by NGF and the American Alliance for Health, Physical Education, Recreation, and Dance (AAHPERD). Many private organizations, such as Golf Digest, offer clinics and schools for private individuals or clubs.

Preparing Your Body For Success

Your body is your most basic piece of equipment. You must warm it up and take care of it, just like you would a great race car. A golfer's body needs to be strong, flexible, and able to endure the 4 to 5 hours of swinging and walking (well over 4 miles).

A warm-up period is needed in golf, as in all other sports. However, the major emphasis of a good golf warm-up is on flexibility and stretching rather than on increasing heart rate. The turning and twisting motion of the golf swing utilizes muscles in various combinations that are not normally exercised each day. For example, the most common injuries in golf occur to the lower back and shoulders due to improper conditioning. Each major muscle group should be systematically stretched: head and neck, shoulders, back (especially lower back), hips, legs (both front and back), and ankles. Hold each stretch for 10 seconds. Repeat 3 to 6 times in both directions. Do not bounce or forcefully twist any body part. Be sure to get a head-to-toe warm-up before each practice session or playing a round. It is also a good idea to do a systematic workout at least three times a week, even when not playing golf.

After stretching well, most golfers go to the practice tee or green. Experiment with which order you prefer. Putting first provides a good confidence builder, followed by hitting some shots with your full swing. This sequence leaves you ready to tee off successfully. On the other hand, some golfers prefer to hit irons and woods first to stretch, and then putt. The order of warm-up practice is a personal thing, but all great golfers warm-up thoroughly.

When you have practiced intensely or after a hot round of golf, it is also important to cool down. Muscles get warm during play and are highly vascularized (increased blood flow) and generally more flexible. Before you put your clubs away, use this time to repeat some of the exercises you worked on for increased range of motion (flexibility). Be sure that when leaving the course or practice tee and going immediately into a cool locker room, 19th-hole snack bar, or air conditioning that you protect your muscles from getting too tight or even cramping. Take time to cool down, or bring a jacket to wear. Remove wet clothing and shower and change to dry clothes as soon as possible.

EQUIPMENT

The ads for golf equipment seen on television, in magazines, and golf shops can be overwhelming and confusing to even the most knowledgeable golfers. The average middle-aged golfer has four putters and at least four drivers stored in a closet somewhere! Whenever something goes wrong with a game, many golfers switch clubs or try a new quick fix.

What clubs are really best and which balls go the farthest? Our attention is most frequently drawn to well-known players such as John Daly, Beth Daniel, and Fred Couples, who have switched club companies (Daly to Wilson, Daniel to Cobra, and Couples to Lynx). Are the clubs that different, or are they being paid more for their services? A little of both is usually the case.

Let's consider some general information on golf equipment and major considerations in getting equipment that is appropriate for you. The two necessities in golf equipment are the club and the ball, both of which are usually transported in a golf bag. Gloves, golf shoes, umbrellas, and other items associated with the game are accessories that can enhance your play, but they are not requirements for learning or playing the game of golf.

Golf Clubs

A set of golf clubs is generally composed of 14 clubs: nine irons, four woods, and a putter. The irons generally range from a 3-iron to a 9-iron, a pitching wedge (PW), and a sand wedge (SW). The woods range from a 1-wood, or a driver, to a 7-wood. Some manufacturers even make a set of 15 woods. Figure 18 shows a selected variety of clubs available.

Irons and woods vary in shaft length and the loft (backward slant) of the clubface, which determine shot distance and trajectory. As the numbers increase, the loft increases and the shaft length decreases. This makes for higher trajectories over shorter distances. The lower the number and the longer the shaft, the greater the potential distance and the flatter, or lower, the trajectory.

Initially a beginner's set might include a 5- or 7-wood, 3-iron, 5-iron, 7-iron, 9-iron, PW, SW, and a putter. Clubs can often be rented or purchased at golf courses. Clubs can be purchased from club professionals, discount centers, sporting good shops, and department stores in a variety of styles and for a variety of prices. The choice of club brand depends on the aesthetic appeal of the club to you, the characteristics of the club's actions, and what is available within your price range. Be sure to consult your instructor, local golf professional, or dealer for assistance.

Your major concern in obtaining clubs should be that they are appropriate for your height, hand size, and strength. Clubs come in assorted sizes and should be fit to you—not you to them. Clubs that are either too short or too long, are too light or too heavy, or have grips that are too small or too large can inhibit your ability to learn the game effectively, no matter what your ability or interest.

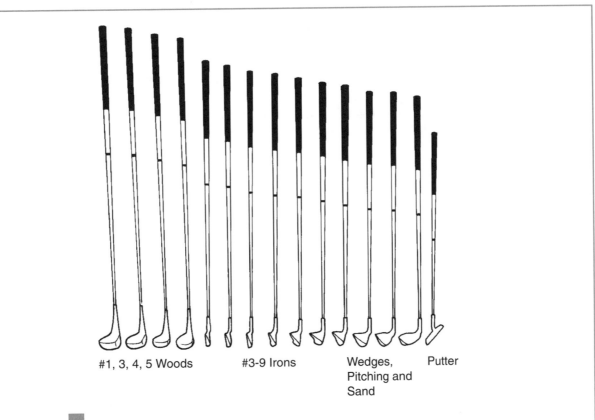

Figure 18 Types of clubs.

It is important that you know your clubs and can refer to them with the appropriate names and terms for the various parts. Figure 19 illustrates the parts of the club.

Woods

Two types of woods are on the market today: the traditional wood and the metal wood. Traditional woods are solid hardwood (e.g., persimmon), or made of laminated wood that is

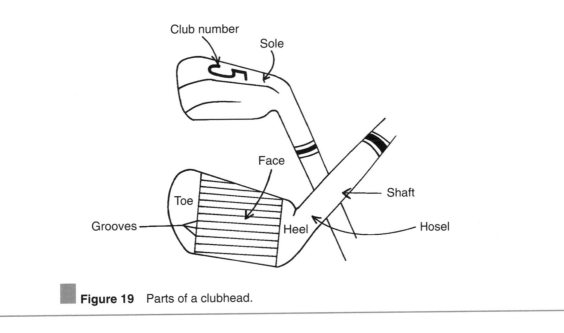

Figure 19 Parts of a clubhead.

less expensive and equally effective for most golfers. Both types of woods are numbered 1 through 7.

Metal woods have become popular since the late 1970s and have been nicknamed "Pittsburgh Persimmon." When compared with traditional woods, metal woods have an advantage in producing speed and control. The harder surface from which the ball rebounds and the more equal weight distribution provide for greater consistency in ball flight control. The smaller hosel design reduces wind resistance, thereby increasing clubhead speed.

Irons

Irons are numbered 1 through 9 and also include the sand wedge, pitching wedge, and loft wedge, a specialty club for more advanced players. There are two basic iron head constructions: the traditional forged iron and the more recent casted iron. The casted iron is less expensive because there are fewer steps in the production and it tends to be more forgiving to less than perfect hits.

There are some differences between irons and the way they look and perform (see Figure 20). For example, some clubs, called perimeter weighted, are better balanced between the heel and toe, while others have less weight distributed to the heel and toe the farther away from the center of the blade. The perimeter weighted clubs tend to be more accurate and provide better distance. To the beginner and average player there are also low-profile irons, which are heavier in the sole, or bottom, to help get the ball airborne and travel at a higher trajectory. Some irons also have a wider, flatter sole, which reduces its normal digging effect.

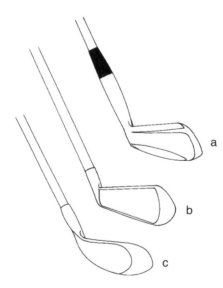

Figure 20 Club designs for irons: (a) traditional, (b) heel-toe weight distribution, (c) sole weighting.

Match Your Clubs to You and Your Golf Game

Some golf club companies only provide two standard types of clubs, men's and women's. Other companies are taking a more modern approach and providing fitting systems that allow you to find the club best for you.

Length of Clubs

The size of club that is perfect for you depends upon many different factors, including your height, length of arms, preferred posture when hitting a ball, and club loft. Because of these complex variables, you should seek the help of your teacher or pro to determine which clubs are best for you at this stage.

Grips

Because your hands are the only things that directly control the club, it is important that the grip on your club is appropriate for you. Grips are made with a variety of materials and textures—leather, rubber, smooth, rough. The type of grip you choose is solely your personal preference, so try several different types. Samples are usually available in golf pro shops for this purpose.

Your grip should fit your hand size (see Figure 21). Hold the club by the grip; the recommended fit is one in which the middle finger of your target-side (upper) hand just touches the palm. If your grip is too large or too small, it affects your hand action and your ability to control the club.

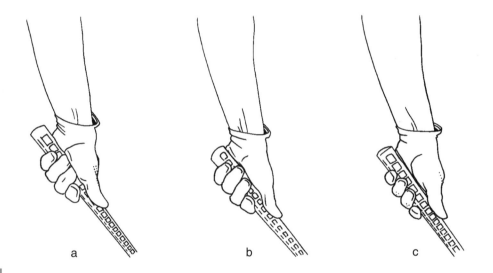

a   b   c

Figure 21 Grip size: (a) too small—palm of hand overlaps fingers; (b) proper fit—index finger of target hand touches the palm; (c) too large—space between the fingers and the palm.

Other Characteristics of Golf Clubs

Golf clubs come with different amounts of flexibility in their shafts, and with different overall weights. In general, you should seek the aid of a golf professional or teacher to assist in fitting your clubs to you.

Many different shafts are available today; they are made of a variety of metals, alloys, and other materials (e.g., graphite, titanium, steel, and fiberglass) and with different weights and amounts of flexibility. Flexibility refers to the amount of bending in the shaft and is rated by letters (A,B,C,D), by numbers (1,2,3,4), or simply by words (from very flexible to extra stiff). The degree of flexibility affects your ability to control the club. The shaft flexibility you need depends on your strength and swing speed. Generally, a golfer who is stronger or has faster swings can accommodate a stiffer shaft. The majority of players' needs fall within the "regular" range of shaft flexibility.

Golf clubs can also vary in swing weight, or overall weight. *Swing weight* refers to the club's weight distribution from the grip to the head of the club. Most clubs are rated from C to D, though the range is from A to E. A club with an overall weight that is too light or too heavy is difficult to control during the swing, and this affects shot distance and accuracy.

Golf Balls

Golf balls come in many varieties—from the internal configuration to the outside cover and color. The internal construction of balls varies from a wound center to a solid, one-piece ball. Covers vary from a softer balata material to a firmer surlyn material. A one-piece ball with a surlyn cover has an edge on distance because it tends to roll more as it hits the ground, and it is more durable. The Spalding Top Flight and Pinnacle by Titleist are among these popular balls. You will hear the commentators during a golf telecast speak of the amount of backspin a player created as her ball hit the green. The Tour players and low handicap golfers prefer the wound construction with the "balata" cover because this ball has a softer cover that gives more on club contact and creates more backspin. As it hits the ground, the ball rolls less than the solid construction ball because of the backspin. Players can also control the spin of the ball more easily allowing them to hit a greater array of shots.

The solid golf ball construction is more durable and has a distance edge. Thus, the solid ball is recommended for most beginning and intermediate golfers. The type of ball construction is not indicated on the ball itself but often on the packages in which it is sold. If you are in doubt, be sure to ask.

Initially, you want a durable ball. The solid ball is more resistant to cuts as the club contacts the ball and will last longer. The slight advantage in distance is nice too! Most ball companies have a variety of balls. You may also want to check at the course you play for "experienced balls." These are balls from the lakes or lost balls that are in good condition, but up for resale. You don't need new balls or the most expensive ones when practicing.

Golf Shoes

Golf shoes are recommended as you begin to practice and play. They provide better traction, which helps you in learning good footwork and weight transfer. Golf shoes are also important as you walk the course and practice for extended periods of time because of the better support provided as compared to tennis shoes. However, tennis shoes are fine initially, especially those that give you good lateral (side) support.

Golf shoes come in various textures of leather, from soft to firm. Less support and stability is provided by the softer leather and such shoes tend to wear out quicker. If you walk and pull a cart or carry your bag as you play, waterproof shoes are available.

Another consideration in selecting golf shoes is whether you want them with or without spikes (i.e. "spikeless"). Shoes with spikes provide better stability during wet conditions and on uneven terrain.

Golf Gloves

A golf glove is beneficial if your hands tend to perspire or if they are soft or easily irritated. The glove is generally worn on the target-side hand and can be made of any one of several styles and fabrics. Whether you wear a golf glove is a matter of personal preference.

STEP 1

SWING MOTION: DEVELOPING FEEL, RHYTHM, AND TEMPO

Television has allowed the game of golf to take on new dimensions. Analysts such as Johnny Miller and Judy Rankin, both former tour professionals, help you understand what the players are thinking as they prepare to execute shots. Then they analyze their swings to let you know what they did or did not do to be successful. Although you should listen to these tips, you should not assume they all apply to your game.

Most players have similar swings. Different physical characteristics can cause some variation among motions, but they are far more similar than different. The swings of Lee Trevino and Jo Anne Carner appear very different; however, their swings have a characteristic *swinging* motion. Other players with excellent swings to emulate are Beth Daniel, Payne Stewart, Tina Barrette, and Tom Kite. Each has a sound setup, and the various aspects of their individual swings are consistent.

Your first basic golf skill to learn is the swing motion, which is the foundation for the golf swing. In this step you learn to control your pivot or body motion, arm swing, and wrist cock by practicing without a club and ball (which will be added in Steps 2 and 3). Once you have learned the swing motion, it will be easy to alter the length and swing pace to produce a variety of other swings needed in golf. By learning the swing first, you'll also be able to detect slight variations in your body posture and tension in executing any golf swing. The swing motion can be learned best using a mirror, so you might want to practice this step indoors.

Why is the Swing Motion Important?

The swing is used on all shots from the teeing area, the starting point for each hole, through shots near the green. It is used with all of the woods and irons and with short shots around the green. The fundamental aspects of the swing stay the same, but the length and pace of the swing vary depending on the shot and club.

How to Execute the Swing Motion

The key to developing a good golf swing is to understand that it is basically a simple swinging motion. Imagine the motion of a pendulum or a swing in the park (see Figure 1.1). The motion is continuous and creates an arc around a center. The center for your golf swing is your sternum (i.e., your breastbone).

An important concept to remember as you begin to learn the golf swing is that the ball merely "gets in the way" of the swinging motion. In golf, the ball remains stationary, so your main objective is to develop a consistent swing. The terrain will vary and obstacles may get in the way, but with slight changes in your setup to the ball, the swing motion will remain fairly constant. In sports such as tennis, volleyball, and racquetball, the objective is to hit a moving ball, which requires developing body positions

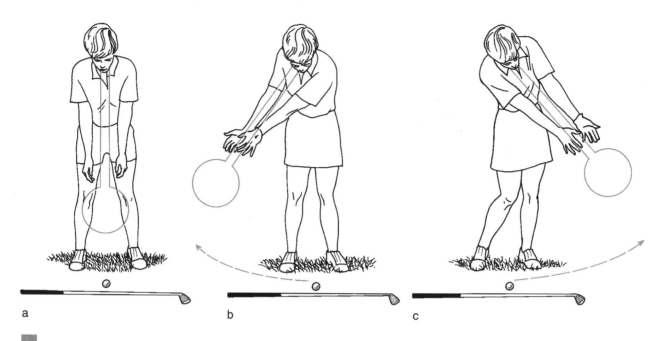

Figure 1.1 The golf swing as a pendulum.

and swing adaptations to adjust for the speed and direction of the moving ball.

When describing a golf swing, it's common to use terms that refer to the *target* and the *phases* of the swing. When you hit a golf ball, you stand sideways to the target. If you are right-handed, your left side is closest to the hole and is called your *target side*, whereas your right arm and leg are on the *rear side*. If you are left-handed, your target side is the right side of your body, and your rear side is your left side. Using the terms target side and rear side allows you to use this book equally well whether you are a right- or left-handed golfer. Finally, rather than always using the word "side" when referring to body parts, we'll sometimes simply use target and rear, as in "target knee" (short for target-side knee) or "rear foot" (for rear-side foot).

The golf swing has three phases: preparation, execution, and follow-through. The preparation phase, or preswing setup position, is the ready position from which you begin to swing. To take your setup position, pick an imaginary target and place a club on the ground pointing to this target. The line from club to target is called a *target line*. In your mind, draw a line parallel to the target line, with about 2-1/2 feet between the two lines. Stand with your toes on the nearest parallel line, feet shoulder width apart, in a square stance (see Figure 1.2a). Bend forward from the top of your thighs at an angle of about 45 de-

grees, keeping your back straight. Let your arms hang relaxed from your shoulders. In a mirror, your hands would be over your toes and under your shoulders. Maintaining this position, flex your knees slightly (see Figure 1.2b). Feel your weight distributed evenly between both feet. Center your weight between the midstep and the balls of your feet so that you can more easily tap your heels than your toes. From this position your swing will follow a circular path. Imagine an inclined wagon wheel on edge in front of you on the ground, with the edge aligned toward your target and the wheel tilted toward you about 45 degrees, forming an "inclined plane." At address in the preparation phase, the ball is at the bottom of your imaginary wheel (see Figure 1.2c).

The execution phase is the actual swing motion, consisting of the backswing and forwardswing. The *backswing* is the motion away from the ball and the *forwardswing* is the motion through the ball. The swing motion is composed of a pivot, an arm swing, and wrist motion. These three elements are independent actions blended in sequence, just like throwing a ball or using a recipe to cook.

The *pivot* is the turning motion of the body or torso about the spine on both the backswing (see Figure 1.3a) and forwardswing (see Figure 1.4a). During the backswing pivot, turn your upper body to the rear with the spine as its axis. The hips should not move yet.

FIGURE
1.2

KEYS TO SUCCESS

PREPARATION PHASE

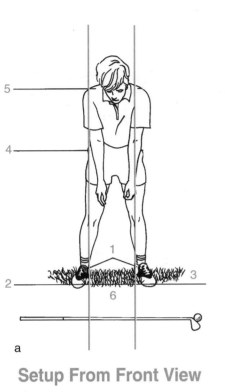

a

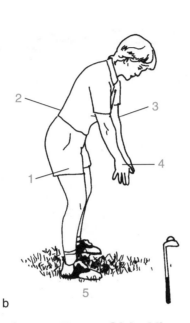

b

c

Setup From Front View

1. Feet shoulder width apart___
2. Stand on imaginary line ___
3. Square foot alignment ___
4. Square hip alignment ___
5. Square shoulder alignment ___
6. Weight even on both feet ___

Setup From Side View

1. Bend from top of thighs ___
2. Posture with flat back ___
3. Arms hang relaxed ___
4. Palms of hands facing each other ___
5. Weight forward, midsteps to balls of feet ___

Inclined Wheel Image

1. Ideal swing will follow a circular path along an inclined plane ___

Start the backswing by moving your hands, arms, and pivot as a unit, being sure to maintain your posture as you coil back into *half-backswing position* (see Figure 1.3b). Your arms are extending away from the target as your body is turning. Your upper arms remain lightly touching the sides of your chest during the first half of the backswing. Your wrists are cocked with your thumbs coming toward the sides of your forearm as shown in the inset in Figure 1.3b.

You will feel you have turned your upper body to position over your rear leg. You'll also feel more weight on your rear side. Your target arm is parallel to the target line; your rear arm is beginning to extend. The back of your target hand is facing the target line. Your hips, turned and facing the target line, remain still until your hands reach about hip height. The upper body pivot then begins to pull the hips, which initiates the lower body pivot.

When your hands are even with or slightly above your hips, your target arm should be parallel to the target line and your rear arm bent slightly. Your shoulders are almost fully turned. At this point, your arms continue to swing up to full backswing posi-tion, your rear arm bending and your target arm extended to just above your rear shoulder (see Figure 1.3c). Your shoulders continue to turn to 90 degrees or to the point your flexibility allows. Your wrists are fully cocked as shown in the inset for Figure 1.3c.

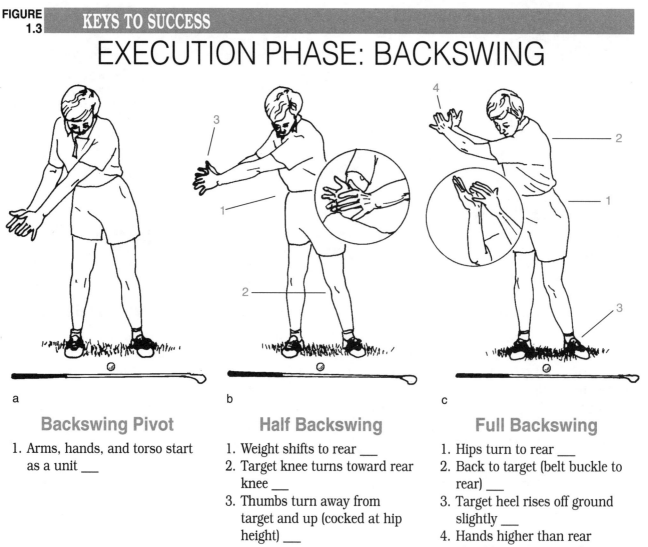

FIGURE 1.3

KEYS TO SUCCESS

EXECUTION PHASE: BACKSWING

a

Backswing Pivot

1. Arms, hands, and torso start as a unit ___

b

Half Backswing

1. Weight shifts to rear ___
2. Target knee turns toward rear knee ___
3. Thumbs turn away from target and up (cocked at hip height) ___

c

Full Backswing

1. Hips turn to rear ___
2. Back to target (belt buckle to rear) ___
3. Target heel rises off ground slightly ___
4. Hands higher than rear shoulder with wrists fully cocked ___

The forwardswing pivot reverses the sequence, with the lower body (i.e., target knee) turning toward the target and the upper body following (see Figure 1.4a). The forwardswing begins with the target knee moving laterally toward the target and the arms pulling down. There is a sense that the rear arm is getting longer, thus maintaining the same arc width as your backswing. Allow your rear knee to turn into your target knee as your arms and hands extend through the bottom of your swing (see Figure 1.4b). As your weight shifts and your hips turn toward the target, momentum pulls your forwardswing into a half follow-through position (see Figure 1.4c).

FIGURE 1.4

KEYS TO SUCCESS

EXECUTION PHASE: FORWARDSWING

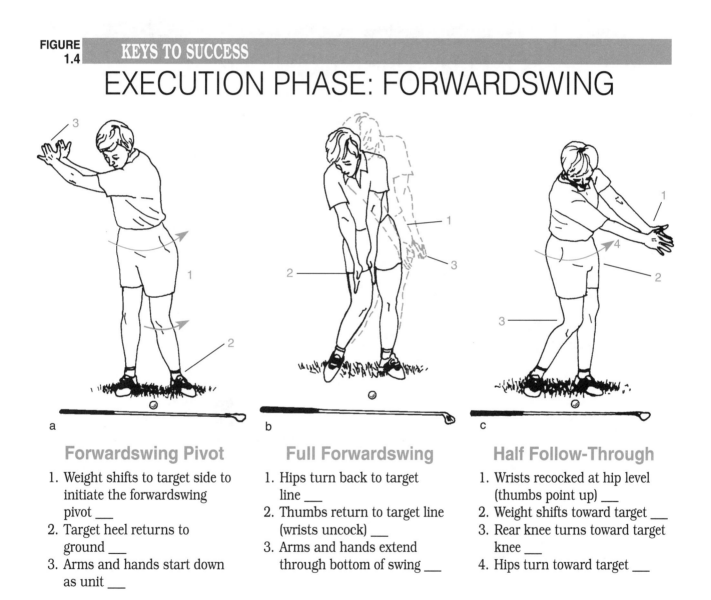

Forwardswing Pivot

1. Weight shifts to target side to initiate the forwardswing pivot __
2. Target heel returns to ground __
3. Arms and hands start down as unit __

Full Forwardswing

1. Hips turn back to target line __
2. Thumbs return to target line (wrists uncock) __
3. Arms and hands extend through bottom of swing __

Half Follow-Through

1. Wrists recocked at hip level (thumbs point up) __
2. Weight shifts toward target __
3. Rear knee turns toward target knee __
4. Hips turn toward target __

The follow-through is the completion point of the swing—the *finish* as it is often called. The hips finish facing the target, having turned more through than back due to the rear knee motion. The shoulders also tend to turn more through than back. The rear shoulder will be closer to the target than the target shoulder. You will be balanced and have a feeling of standing tall (see Figure 1.5).

Follow all three phases of the golf swing shown in Figures 1.2 through 1.5. Remember that it is necessary to first learn the full swing motion without a club or ball.

FIGURE
1.5

KEYS TO SUCCESS

FOLLOW-THROUGH PHASE

Finish

1. Weight on target side ___
2. Rear knee toward target side ___
3. Hips face target (belt buckle toward target) ___
4. Chest toward target ___
5. Arms and hands higher than shoulder ___
6. Balanced ending ___

SWING MOTION SUCCESS STOPPERS

The desired posture and swing motion is easier to recognize when compared to undesired techniques. The most common errors are presented below, along with suggestions on how to correct them.

ERROR	CORRECTION
1. You sit too far back on your heels (can tap toes without losing balance).	1. Bend forward from top of thighs. Center weight over midsteps to balls of feet (tap heels, not toes).
2. On backswing, weight stays on target side; does not shift to rear side.	2. Shift weight to rear side by moving target knee into rear knee.
3. Thumbs point to ground on half follow-through.	3. Turn arms and hands as they swing downward through ball; thumbs should point to sky at follow-through (see Figures 1.3c and 1.4c).

SWING MOTION

DRILLS

1. Posture Drill

Practice taking the desired posture by holding a club vertically along your spine. The club should touch your head and extend below your waist. Slowly bend forward from the top of your thighs. When the club comes off your head or back, you have bent forward too far.

Success Goal = 5 repetitions with club down back and correct posture _____

Success Check
• Feel bend from top of the thighs _____

To Increase Difficulty
• Hold club with one hand only.

2. Body Rotation Drill

To feel your body rotate and your weight shift, take your setup position. With both hands, hold a club in front and across your shoulders, the club shaft pointing toward an imaginary target (see Figure a), maintaining the angle of your posture in your setup. Practice your torso and leg movement of the full swing motion so that on the backswing one club end points forward; at the end of your forwardswing, the opposite end should point forward over the position of the ball (see Figure b). Notice how your shoulders and club align perpendicular to the incline angle to form a T (see Figure c).

Success Goal = 15 total body rotations
5 rotations, eyes open ____
5 rotations, eyes closed ____
5 rotations, eyes open again ____

Success Check
• Maintain angle of posture during setup ____
• Rotate so that shaft points toward ball ____
• Feel stretch across your back ____

a   b   c

3. Half-Swing Practice Drill

Take your setup posture, palms facing each other. Place a club on the ground for the target line (see Figure 1.2). Practice half-swings.

Success Goal = 7 half-swings with desired form ____

To Increase Difficulty
• Using a mirror, alternate eyes open and closed to check position.

Success Check
• Arms lightly touch sides of chest ____
• Feel arms extended down, body turns ____
• Maintain posture ____

4. Arm Swing and Pivot Drill

Find a partner to do this drill with. Place your hands about 2 inches to the right and left side of your partner's head. As your partner executes the swing, see the motion around his or her center. The head will move slightly to the rear with the pivot.

Success Goal = 5 repetitions seeing partner's turning around center ____

Success Checks
• Maintain posture throughout swing ____
• Feel pivot, turn around spine ____

To Increase Difficulty
• Swing with eyes closed.

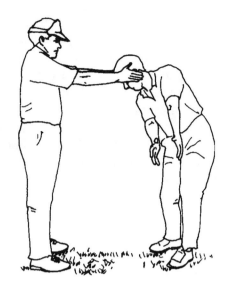

5. Wheel Image Drill

To help conceptualize the swing turn, visualize and/or feel your head as the hub of a wheel and your arms as spokes (see Figure a). Also visualize your body turning around an imaginary rod running down your back. Close your eyes as you practice your swing motion and visualize your body turning with your arms as the spokes of the wheel moving through the 1-to-1 position (see Figures b and c), then 2-to-2, and 3-to-3.

Success Goal = 10 swings with visualizations and/or feel of described form ____

Success Check
• See and/or feel your motion ____

To Increase Difficulty
• Repeat with your eyes open.
• Visualize your swing.

To Decrease Difficulty
• Practice in front of a mirror. See yourself swinging, then close your eyes and repeat what you saw or felt.

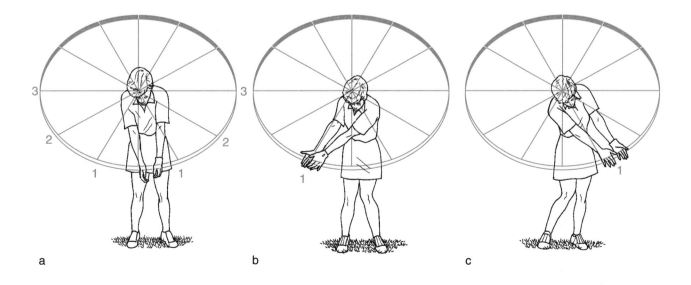

a   b   c

SWING MOTION SUCCESS SUMMARY

Next time you watch golf on television, turn off the sound and just watch the golf swings of the LPGA and PGA players. Note the wholeness of the motion, the rhythm, balance, and tempo. Then focus on the blending of the arm swing with the body motion. There's a specific sequence in the swing: a preparation, backswing, forwardswing, and finish.

Test yourself by checking for the Success Goals in this first step: preparation and setup, backswing and forwardswing, rhythm and timing, and a balanced, symmetrical follow-through. Ask your teacher, your coach, or a friend to evaluate your technique according to the checklist in Figures 1.2 through 1.5, checking off each item seen in your swing.

STEP 2

SETUP AND PRESWING ROUTINE: CONSISTENCY IS THE KEY

As you watch tour professionals and good amateur players, they appear methodical as they prepare to hit each shot. Their posture, discussed in Step 1, appears the same for each shot. The way they place their hands on the club, the distance they set up from the ball, and the placement of the ball in their stance also look the same each time. These procedures are some of the components of the preswing routine (also called the *preshot* routine) and setup position (also called the *ready* position) for hitting shots. Some of these players are deliberate in their preshot routine, such as Tom Kite or Betsy King; others perform the routine quicker, almost fast, such as Lee Trevino and Fuzzy Zoeller. Different methods work for different golfers, and there is no one best way. In time, you'll discover which preshot method works best for you.

In this step, we'll add the club and ball to the swing motion you practiced in Step 1. We'll recommend a preswing routine that you can adapt or modify to match your preferences. As your skill level increases and you learn the different golf shots in later steps, there will be only slight modifications of the swing setup as you develop your own preshot routine.

Why Are the Setup and Preswing Routine Important?

The preswing routine and setup position are the foundation on which your swing is built. Proper posture and relation to the club and ball need to be consistent because your swing depends on these starting points. The preswing routine and setup are fundamental skills that should be practiced like any other skill.

Consistency in your preswing routine and setup position help you develop a more dependable, repeatable swing. Betsy King, an LPGA Player of the Year, leading money winner, and leading scorer is a player noted for consistency in her preswing routine and setup. Although you may not aspire to play the tour, you can still strive to be as consistent in your preparation as tour players. Frequent practice on your preswing routine will program you to take the correct setup position for whatever shot you select. When you are inconsistent in your preswing routine or setup, the resulting swing motion is not as effective in producing the desired shot distance and direction.

How to Execute Your Setup and Preswing Routine

In this section you will further develop the setup position you practiced in Step 1; then you'll combine your setup position with your preswing routine.

The setup position has seven phases: (a) stance, (b) posture, (c) weight distribution, (d) body alignment, (e) grip, (f) ball position, and (g) clubface alignment. In Step 1 you practiced the first four phases as you went through the swing motion. Now you can add the club and ball to practice the ball positioning, grip, and clubface alignment. You'll probably find it helpful to review the full swing Keys to Success in Step 1 (see pp. 27-30).

Grip

The grip position presented here is called the *overlapping neutral grip*. To grip the club, place one hand on the club at a time, beginning with your target hand (see Figure 2.1a). Allow your target hand and arm to hang *relaxed* by your side. With the clubface facing the target, let the club rest in your fingers and close your hand on the club. The club grip will be positioned diagonally across your palm and fingers (see Figure 2.1b). Note the club should rest under the muscle or pad of your hand, above the little finger, not in your palm. Your thumb should rest slightly to the rear side of the club. Looking down at your grip,

you should see two knuckles. Your index finger and thumb should form a V pointing to the rear side of your chin (see Figure 2.1c). There is no gap between your thumb and index finger.

To position your rear hand on the club, grip the club in your target hand and hold the club in front of you (Figure 2.2a). Place your rear hand on the club with the palm facing the target as if you are shaking hands (Figure 2.2b). Hold the club in the fingers of your rear hand, the little finger of your rear hand resting on the index finger of your target hand. Your thumb should rest just to the target side of the club with one knuckle visible. Your index finger and thumb should form a V pointing just to the rear side of your chin (matching the V of your target hand) with no gap between the thumb and index finger (Figures 2.2b and 2.2c).

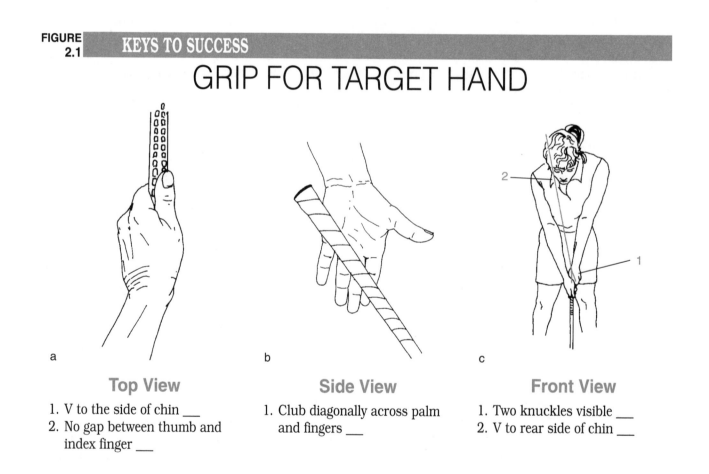

FIGURE 2.1 **KEYS TO SUCCESS**

GRIP FOR TARGET HAND

a **Top View**

1. V to the side of chin ___
2. No gap between thumb and index finger ___

b **Side View**

1. Club diagonally across palm and fingers ___

c **Front View**

1. Two knuckles visible ___
2. V to rear side of chin ___

FIGURE
2.2   KEYS TO SUCCESS

GRIP FOR REAR HAND

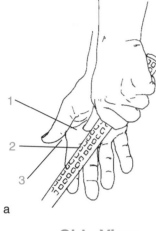

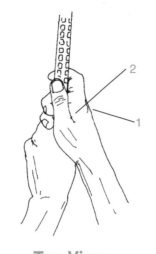

a

b

c

Side View

1. Palm of hand to target ___
2. Club in fingers ___
3. No gap between thumb and index finger ___

Top View

1. One knuckle visible ___
2. No gap between thumb and index finger ___

Front View

1. V to rear side of chin ___

Preswing Routine

To take the setup position with either a wood or an iron, start from directly behind the ball in line with your target. Select an intermediate target about 1 to 3 feet in front of the ball. A blade of grass works well, or a divot—anything you can distinguish. This intermediate target is easier to see and use for alignment than a distant target (see Figure 2.3a). Grip your club in both hands. You may do this from behind the ball or from the side (parallel to your target line). Align according to the ball's position. Stand erect with your feet together and extend your arms, allowing them to rest lightly on your chest. Keeping your back straight, bend from the top of your thighs to a point where the club touches the ground behind the ball and your arms are hanging relaxed. The club should be aligned behind the ball in a position square to the target.

For the full swing using an iron, position the ball about 2 inches target side of center in your stance. For a wood, place the ball about 1 inch to the rear side of your target foot. The ball position for the wood is more closely aligned with your target shoulder.

This difference is due to the lengths of the clubs and the intended angle of contacting the ball. The wood is designed to sweep the ground or contact the ball at a shallow angle, whereas the iron contacts the ball at a more downward angle of the club.

For an iron, move your target foot toward the target about 6 inches and your rear foot away from the target about 8 inches. This produces a ball position just to the target side of center in your stance for the iron (see Figure 2.3b).

For a wood, move your target foot, positioning the ball under your target shoulder. Move your rear foot about 14 inches away from the target, which produces a shoulder-width stance (about 16 inches). The ball position is shifted toward the target relative to your body, the center of your body behind the ball (see Figure 2.3b).

The position of the clubface when it is resting behind the ball is called the *clubface alignment*. For almost all shots in golf, the clubface should be perpendicular to the target line (i.e., the desired line of flight of the ball). As you become more advanced, this position can vary to produce different ball flights.

For now, though, be sure that your clubface is square to the target (see Figure 2.3c).

As described in detail in the Equipment section, it is important that your clubs are fit for you. Whenever possible the ideal is to have your clubs fit *to you*. This is called a dynamic club fitting. If a dynamic fit is not possible in your setup position, the bottom of the club should rest flat on the ground. Every club has a nearly flat bottom (the sole) designed to rest on the ground and be most efficient when the full length of the sole contacts the ground at setup. If in your setup position your club rests with the toe or the heel off the ground, you may want to have your teacher or local professional check to be sure that your clubs are the right length and have the right lie for you (i.e., the way the club sets to the ground). If you are over 6 feet tall, or under 5 feet, 5 inches, the standard, off-the-shelf club may not be appropriate for you.

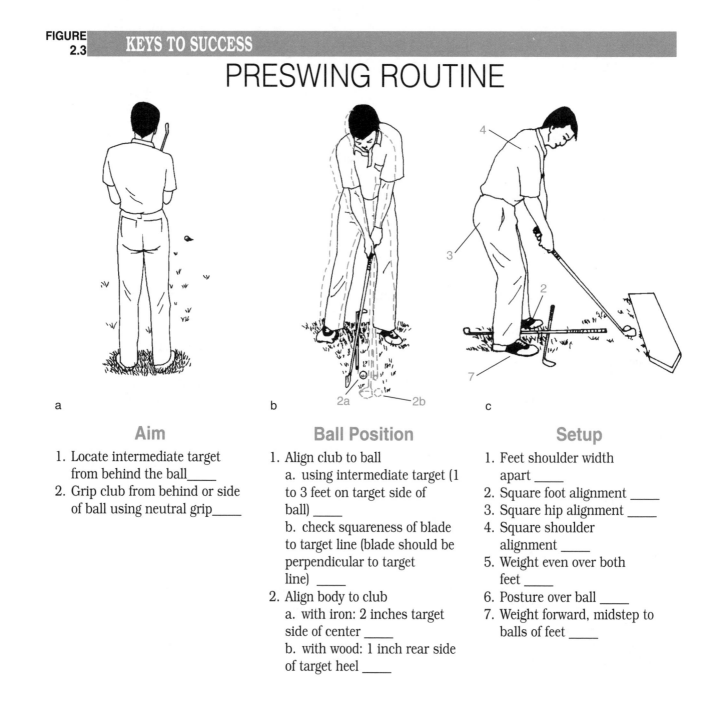

FIGURE 2.3 KEYS TO SUCCESS

PRESWING ROUTINE

a   b   c

Aim

1. Locate intermediate target from behind the ball____
2. Grip club from behind or side of ball using neutral grip____

Ball Position

1. Align club to ball
   a. using intermediate target (1 to 3 feet on target side of ball) ____
   b. check squareness of blade to target line (blade should be perpendicular to target line) ____
2. Align body to club
   a. with iron: 2 inches target side of center ____
   b. with wood: 1 inch rear side of target heel ____

Setup

1. Feet shoulder width apart ____
2. Square foot alignment ____
3. Square hip alignment ____
4. Square shoulder alignment ____
5. Weight even over both feet ____
6. Posture over ball ____
7. Weight forward, midstep to balls of feet ____

SETUP AND PRESWING ROUTINE SUCCESS STOPPERS

Constantly checking your preswing routine and setup position helps you develop consistency in your swing. The most common errors found in the preswing routine and setup are described below, along with suggestions for their correction.

ERROR	CORRECTION
1. You change your target line by realigning your feet after addressing the ball (i.e., you lose your intermediate target).	1. Go back behind ball and check that the proper intermediate target was in focus.
2. You set your body, then align the club.	2. Begin the setup again, aligning your club first; then align your body to the club.
3. Your grip is turned, with Vs formed by index fingers and thumbs pointing outside rear shoulder.	3. Move hands more toward target side so Vs are pointing just to rear side of chin.
4. In setup position, arms stretch out too far, so that a plumb line from eyes would fall onto forearms.	4. Move arms closer to body where plumb line would fall on hands.
5. Using an iron, you position ball too far forward, off your target heel.	5. Practice setting up with an iron by placing a club on ground in middle of stance.
6. You sit back in stance as if you were sitting on a stool or tilting backward; you can tap your toes easily.	6. Bend more from the top of your thighs so weight is over midstep to balls of feet; thus, you can tap heels, not toes.

DRILLS

1. Grip Practice Drill

Practice taking your grip with your eyes closed. Hold your arms straight out in front of your chest, with the club up in the air. Then open your eyes. You can practice this effectively almost anywhere—at home or at the office.

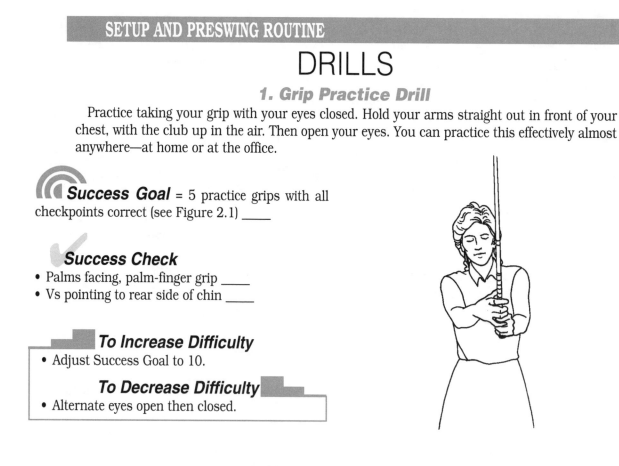

Success Goal = 5 practice grips with all checkpoints correct (see Figure 2.1) ____

Success Check
- Palms facing, palm-finger grip ____
- Vs pointing to rear side of chin ____

To Increase Difficulty
- Adjust Success Goal to 10.

To Decrease Difficulty
- Alternate eyes open then closed.

2. Weight Distribution: Forward and Back Drill

Practice in front of a mirror. First, take your proper stance. Now feel an undesired setup position by leaning back as if you were sitting on a stool. Then look in the mirror. Match what it looks like with the feel. Do your arms feel as relaxed as in the desired position? Next, tip too far forward so your weight is on the balls and toes of your feet. Tap your heels on the ground. Look again in the mirror to see how this position looks. Now find the middle position. Repeat these three positions: back, forward, and balanced.

Success Goal = 3 cycles taking proper stance, then shifting weight backward, too far forward, and back to ideal stance
- 3 setup positions forward ____
- 3 setup positions back ____
- 3 setup positions balanced ____

Success Check
- Arms relaxed and hanging ____
- Slight lean from top of thighs ____
- Tap heels ____

To Increase Difficulty
- Practice with eyes open, then closed.

To Decrease Difficulty
- Alternate between proper stance and either backward or forward tilt and pressure on balls of feet or heels.
- Practice with a two-by-four setup, with heels on board, toes on board, and without board and weight on midstep to balls of feet.

3. Walk Away Alignment Drill

Practice your setup positions by starting behind the ball. Pick an imaginary target, then walk up and take your setup over the ball (review Figures 2.3a-c). Now lay your club on the ground, touching the tips of your toes. Walk back behind ball and look at club to determine whether your toes were parallel to the target line. Pick different targets and repeat.

Success Goal = 7 consecutive correct parallel alignments, each attempt directed at a different target ____

Success Check
• Align club square to target ____
• Set your posture ____

To Increase Difficulty
• Expand Success Goal to include alignment accuracy and meeting all items on Setup checklist 5 of 7 times.

To Decrease Difficulty
• Use an alignment club by the ball; practice drill with an alignment club, then without one.
• Place a tee about 2 feet in front of ball as an alignment guide.

4. Arm Hang Drill

In setup position, release your grip on the club and let it fall away. Let your arms relax, noting whether they remain hanging straight down or swing in toward or away from your body. If your arms swing out, you are too close to the ball. If they fall in toward your body, you are too far from the ball.

Success Goal = 7 arm hangs demonstrating correct relation to ball using a 5-iron ____

Success Check
• Arms and shoulders relaxed ____

To Increase Difficulty
• Alternate between a wood and an iron.

To Decrease Difficulty
• Adjust Success Goal to 5 of 7 correct setups.

5. Intermediate Target Drill

Pick a target in your practice field. Stand behind the ball and select an intermediate target 1 to 3 feet ahead of the ball. Place a piece of tape between the ball and intermediate target and return to the rear of ball to check the line of the target.

Success Goal = 10 alignments with intermediate target in line with target _____

Success Check
• Ball, intermediate target, and target should be in line _____

To Increase Difficulty
• Walk up to ball, walk around it twice, then get into setup position and aim at target. Walk back and check on alignment.

SETUP AND PRESWING ROUTINE SUCCESS SUMMARY

Your preswing routine and setup are the foundation of your swing. They are not the most exciting part of learning the swing, but they are the most important. You can practice your individual preswing routine and setup anywhere. Away from the course, practice is beneficial because you're focusing only on the preswing routine and setup—not the potential outcome of your swing. Use a mirror to self-monitor your setup. During practice, have a friend or teacher check the grip and preswing routine points listed in Figures 2.1 through 2.3.

STEP 3

DISTANCE SWING: HITTING FULL IRONS AND WOODS

The swing motion and the setup position you have been practicing thus far are the foundations for your golf swing. All great golfers have a consistent, repeatable setup and preswing routine. Good alignment and posture are easy to see in great golfers such as Jack Nicklaus, Beth Daniel, Brandy Burton, and Nick Faldo.

In Step 3, you'll now apply your setup and swing motion to actually hitting golf balls with irons and woods. This is called the *full swing* or *distance swing*. In the steps that follow (4 through 9), you'll use your preswing routine, setup, and the swing motion to execute all the other shots needed to play golf. Once you start hitting balls, you may become overly concerned about distance versus accuracy. It is important to start by swinging a full, up-to-tempo swing. Don't worry about pin-point accuracy yet. Focus on developing a fluid, balanced swing.

Why Is the Full Swing Motion Important?

On the golf course, the full swing motion is used for about 50 percent of the shots. So, if you can master this one motion, you'll be halfway to becoming a good golfer!

The game of golf lets you use one consistent swinging motion for most types of shots. Because the design of the golf club largely determines the trajectory and distance of the shot, golfers carry a set of 14 clubs that vary in shape and length. There are many different clubs to be used on any one hole, depending on how far you must hit the ball, the trajectory

needed, and the situation from which the shot starts (e.g., tall grass or sand). Yet, the basic full swing remains the same for every shot. In contrast, the pace of a racket sport such as tennis requires that you play all the shots in a point with a single racket. As a result, for different types of shots, the racket stroke varies considerably. Because the golfer can switch to the ideal club for the shot, there is no need to vary the swing. Having such a wide selection of clubs allows you to rely and concentrate on a single, consistent swinging motion for most types of shots.

As previously discussed in the equipment section, each club is designed to hit the ball in a way that makes it fly higher or lower and cover shorter or longer distances. In general, the higher the number of a club, the higher the ball's trajectory and the shorter the overall distance. The trajectories shown in Figure 3.1 illustrate how the various clubs produce different flight distances and trajectories even though you hit every shot with the same full swing. Compare the distances and trajectories of the 3-wood (sometimes used in place of a driver) and the 9-iron (a short iron). The 3-wood hits the ball farther with a lower trajectory; in contrast, the 9-iron makes the ball fly higher for a shorter distance.

No two golfers using a given club hit the ball the same distance because each person has different skills and strength in accelerating the club throughout the swing (as will be discussed in Step 4). For example, in a group of four beginning golfers, if all four were about 150 yards from the hole, each player might hit a different club. Some might hit a wood and others an iron, depending on individual swing characteristics (i.e., how fast they swing the club and

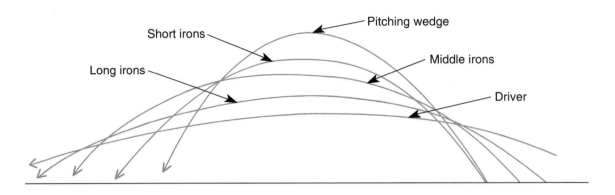

Figure 3.1 Ball flight trajectories produced with a full swing, depending on the club.

how accurate they are) and their preferences for using one club over another. In each case, though, a full swing motion would be applied.

How to Execute the Full Swing Motion

The same full swing motion and basic setup position are used for both irons and woods. The only difference between hitting irons and woods is the ball placement. For irons, the ball is positioned within 1 or 2 inches forward of center of your stance. For woods, the ball is about 1 to 2 inches to the rear side of the target heel, under the target shoulder. Your ideal ball position can be found by taking your setup position with the club touching the ground just forward of the center of your stance for an iron, and just to the rear side of your target heel for the woods. Then take one or two practice swings without a ball. Watch where the club consistently contacts the ground with each swing arc, where the club will contact the bottom of the ball. This is your ball position.

As you are learning the full swing motion, your ball contact and ball flight direction may be inconsistent. Don't worry about that for now. Concentrate on feeling the swinging motion. The motion of your arms, hands, and pivot swinging the club is rhythmic and free. The sequence of movements presented in Step 1 and the Keys to Success in Figures 3.2a-1 should flow smoothly and uninterrupted by any sudden surge of power or forced effort.

FIGURE
3.2

KEYS TO SUCCESS

FULL SWING MOTION WITH CLUBS

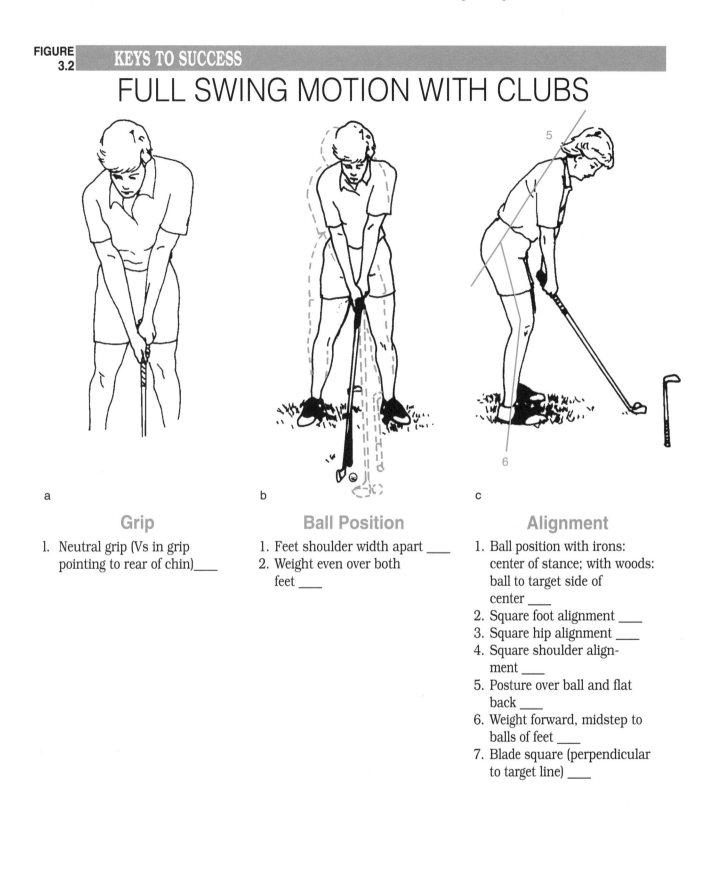

a

b

c

Grip

1. Neutral grip (Vs in grip pointing to rear of chin)____

Ball Position

1. Feet shoulder width apart ____
2. Weight even over both feet ____

Alignment

1. Ball position with irons: center of stance; with woods: ball to target side of center ____
2. Square foot alignment ____
3. Square hip alignment ____
4. Square shoulder alignment ____
5. Posture over ball and flat back ____
6. Weight forward, midstep to balls of feet ____
7. Blade square (perpendicular to target line) ____

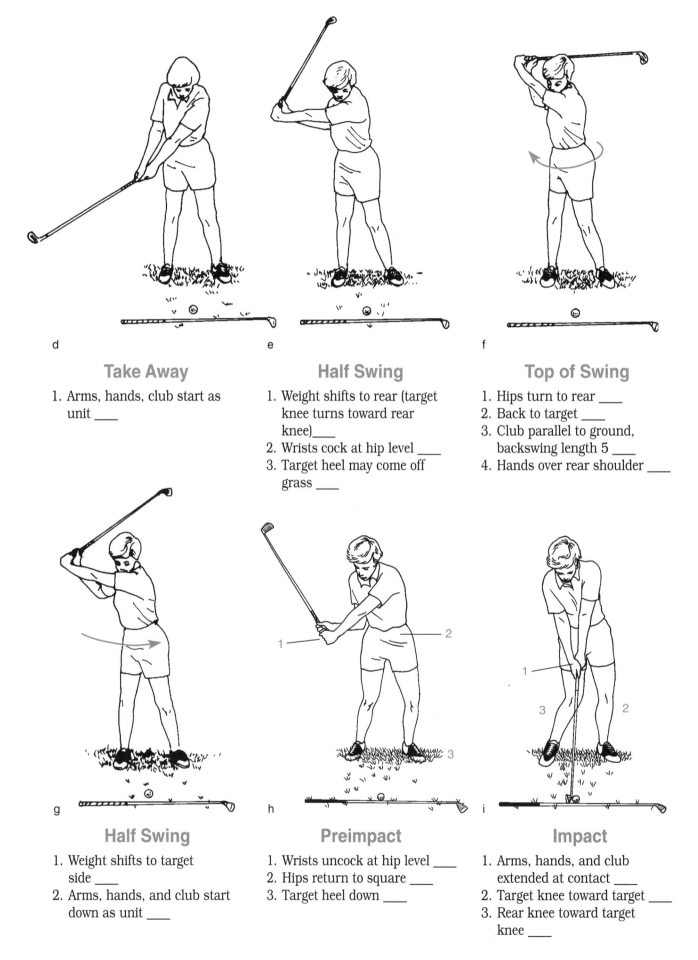

d

Take Away

1. Arms, hands, club start as unit ___

e

Half Swing

1. Weight shifts to rear (target knee turns toward rear knee)___
2. Wrists cock at hip level ___
3. Target heel may come off grass ___

f

Top of Swing

1. Hips turn to rear ___
2. Back to target ___
3. Club parallel to ground, backswing length 5 ___
4. Hands over rear shoulder ___

g

Half Swing

1. Weight shifts to target side ___
2. Arms, hands, and club start down as unit ___

h

Preimpact

1. Wrists uncock at hip level ___
2. Hips return to square ___
3. Target heel down ___

i

Impact

1. Arms, hands, and club extended at contact ___
2. Target knee toward target ___
3. Rear knee toward target knee ___

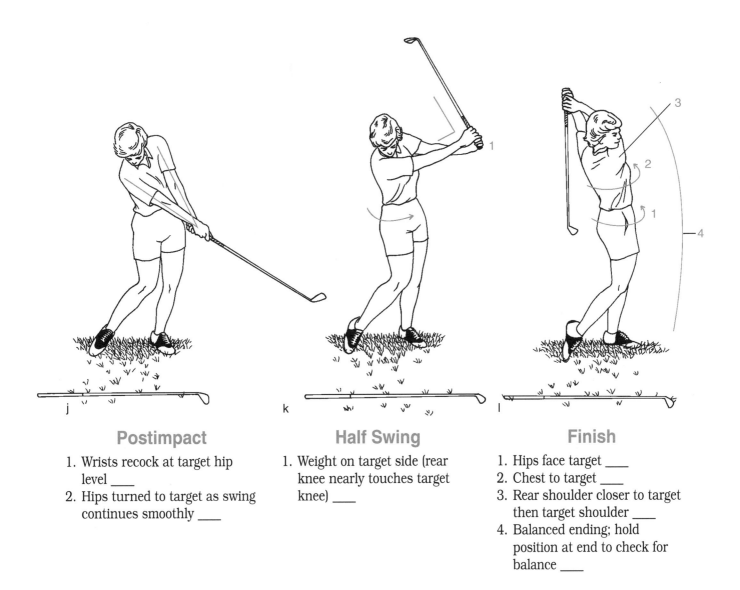

Postimpact

1. Wrists recock at target hip level ___
2. Hips turned to target as swing continues smoothly ___

Half Swing

1. Weight on target side (rear knee nearly touches target knee) ___

Finish

1. Hips face target ___
2. Chest to target ___
3. Rear shoulder closer to target then target shoulder ___
4. Balanced ending; hold position at end to check for balance ___

Imagine a child swinging in the park. The swing's chains represent your arms, and the child and seat represent your hands and club. The upward motion is smooth but gradually slows down. There is an almost imperceptible pause at the height of the upward motion. As the swing starts back on the forward motion, a gradual acceleration continues *through* the lowest part of the swing's arc as the swing comes close to the ground and begins to swing upward. Once the swing passes the bottom of the arc, the swing begins a natural, gradual deceleration. Imagine that your swing feels like the rhythmic swing in the park.

FULL SWING MOTION SUCCESS STOPPERS

The most common problems in a full swing are made obvious by improper contact with the ball. These errors are listed below, along with suggestions on how to correct them.

ERROR	CORRECTION
1. Club hits ground behind ball as your weight shifts.	1. a. Keep arms swinging through ball. b. Maintain posture through impact. c. Review arm swing drills.
2. Club hits top of ball.	2. a. Keep arms extended toward ground on forwardswing. b. Check arm extension as wrists uncock toward ball.
3. You hit ball off toe of club.	3. Maintain posture over ball. Avoid "standing up" or shifting weight back onto heels during forwardswing.
4. You *shank* ball, hitting it off heel of club.	4. Check setup for relaxed arms; be sure your arms are not stretched too far away from your body or leaning forward beyond the ball (see correction 3).
5. Lack of shot distance with full swings due to not turning hips.	5. Take practice swings to feel full body turn and arm swing during both backswing and follow-through. Think "belt buckle back and belt buckle through."
6. Ball travels straight but ends up off target.	6. Check alignment (aim) using Walk Away Alignment Drill (#3) in Step 2 to check for square alignment; do Drill 4 in Step 1 to check arm swing.
7. You swing and miss ball (called a *whiff*).	7. a. Check that posture remains same throughout swing. b. Maintain arm extension through forwardswing.

FULL SWING MOTION

DRILLS

1. Wide Whoosher Drill

To feel the freedom of the arm swing, hold a club upside down in your target hand just above the hosel (the socket in the clubhead for the shaft). Turn the club parallel to the ground, the grip pointing away from an imaginary target. Grip the club shaft with the fingers of your rear hand, palm up, about 1 foot from your target hand.

Take your setup position with the club parallel to the ground (see Figure a). Make your full swing motion to the top of the backswing (see Figure b). Let go with your rear hand and pull down and through with your target-side arm and hand (see Figure c). The club should make a swishing or whooshing sound. If it doesn't, you're not accelerating the swing of the club fast enough through the ball. (Review Drill 4, Step 1.) Begin swinging slowly to get the feel of the motion. Gradually increase the speed.

Success Goal = 10 swings with a loud whooshing sound ____

Success Check
• Listen to the "whoosh" sound ____

To Increase Difficulty
• Swing with target arm only.
• Place rear hand on the back hip and push forward to start forwardswing and exaggerate feel of hip turn.

To Decrease Difficulty
• Decrease reps to 10.
• Use a shorter club.

a   b   c

2. Wheel Image Without a Ball Drill

To get a feel for the pendulum motion of the full swing, imagine that your arms and hands together gripping a club are the spoke of a wheel. The length of your backswing and forwardswing are represented on each side of the wheel by the numbers 1 through 5. Zero is the ball and the setup position of the clubhead.

Practice-swing a 5-iron and a 5-wood in a very short arc, from backswing position 1 to forwardswing position 1. Allow the club to brush the ground on each forwardswing. Now swing the club 2 to 2, 3 to 3, 4 to 4, and 5 to 5. Be sure your swing is the same length on the backswing as on the forwardswing. Sense how the feel of the swing matched how long it is.

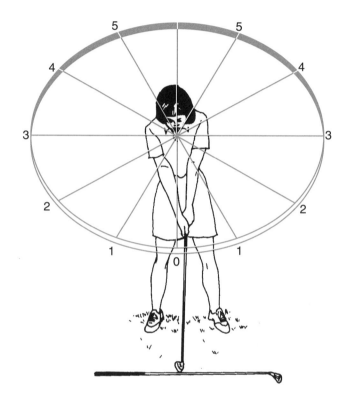

Success Goal = 10 total swings

2 swings, 1-to-1 swing length (no wrist cock) _____

2 swings, 2-to-2 swing length (no wrist cock) _____

2 swings, 3-to-3 swing length (wrists cock) _____

2 swings, 4-to-4 swing length (wrists cock) _____

2 swings, 5-to-5 swing length (wrists cock) _____

✔ **Success Check**

• Maintain posture through impact _____
• Feel unit hands, arms pivot _____
• Feel stretch on backswing _____

To Increase Difficulty

• Practice with your eyes closed.
• Alternate swing lengths as follows: 5 to 5, 2 to 2, 4 to 4, 1 to 1, and 3 to 3.

To Decrease Difficulty

• Practice in front of a mirror, checking your swing lengths.
• Practice only 5-to-5 and 3-to-3 swing lengths.

3. Wheel Image With a Ball Drill

a. Visualize the wheel practiced with the previous drill. Using a 5- or 7-iron and a ball placed on a tee (about one finger's width high), hit balls with each of the swing lengths. Match the feel of the swing with the distance that the ball travels.

b. Repeat Step a without a tee. Be sure the ball is on top of the ground or on grass—not in a divot hole.

Success Goal =

a. 25 total swings, ball elevated on a tee
5 swings, 4-to-4 swing length ____
5 swings, 3-to-3 swing length ____
5 swings, 1-to-1 swing length ____
5 swings, 2-to-2 swing length ____
5 swings, 5-to-5 swing length ____
b. 25 total swings, ball resting on ground (no tee)
5 swings, 3-to-3 swing length ____
5 swings, 1-to-1 swing length ____
5 swings, 4-to-4 swing length ____
5 swings, 2-to-2 swing length ____
5 swings, 5-to-5 swing length ____

To Increase Difficulty

• Alternate using a 5- and 7-iron and a 5- or 7-wood for each swing length.
• Alternate swing lengths and clubs as follows: 5 to 5, 3 to 3, 1 to 1, and 2 to 2.
• Expand Success Goal to include accuracy within 15 yards right and left of selected target.

To Decrease Difficulty

• Practice with club of your choice.

Success Check

• Maintain posture ____
• Feel unit ____
• Coil back, uncoil through the ball ____

4. Cocking Wrists Motion Drill

This drill helps you feel the maximum wrist cock, uncock, and recock you would ever desire on the backswing or forwardswing. Place a club on the ground for your target line and assume your setup position. Without swinging your arms, cock your wrists back so they point to the sky. This is your maximum wrist cock (see Figure a).

a. With a 7-iron, take your stance with your feet close together. Without swinging your arms, turn your thumbs away from the target, back to the ball, and then toward the target. The forearms turn as the thumbs turn.

b. Add a 3-to-3 arm swing arc, the hand action created by the cocking and uncocking of your wrists (see Figures b and c). Note the swinging sensations in your arms and hands.

c. Take your normal stance and setup with your feet shoulder width apart. Add the pivot backward and uncoil the ball through.

Success Goal = 20 total swings using swing cue word (as in Wide Whoosher Drill) each time. Take your normal setup.

a. 5 swings of cocking, uncocking, and recocking using wrists only (without swinging arms) ____
b. 5 swings of 3-to-3 swing length, adding arms and pivot with wrists ____
c. 5 swings of 3-to-3 swing length, adding arms and pivot with wrists and hitting balls from a tee ____
d. 5 swings of 3-to-3 swing length, adding arms and pivot with wrists and hitting balls without a tee ____

✔ Success Check

- Imagine the inclined wheel ____
- Shaft end of the club (i.e., butt of club) toward the target line ____
- Angle of the shaft matches on the backswing and forwardswing ____

To Increase Difficulty

- Include an accuracy element when the balls are hit off a tee (e.g., the ball landing within 15 yards to the right or left of a designated target).
- Increase the swings when hitting balls to 9, and alternate shots with a 5-, 7-, and 9-iron.

To Decrease Difficulty

- Reduce total swings to 12 (3 in each condition).
- Use a tee for all balls hit.

3-to-3 arm swing arc

5. Shadow Drill

When practicing outside, whether at home or at a range, your shadow can be like having your own video. You can see and feel your swing at the same time. For this drill, you'll want to face your shadow directly and take your setup position with an iron or wood of your choice. Place the ball in the middle of your head's shadow, which will be in the middle of your stance. Practice your swing, keeping your head's shadow on the ball. Your head will move slightly to the rear side as you pivot back and to the target side as you move through impact to the finish.

⌒ Success Goal = 8 total swings focusing on seeing and feeling your pivot

a. 3 swings focusing on seeing your swing ____
b. 3 swings seeing and feeling your swing ____
c. 2 swings either seeing, feeling, or seeing and feeling your swing ____

✔ Success Check

- See your pivot ____
- See and feel your pivot ____

To Increase Difficulty

- Use the One-Leg Toe Drill (Drill 7) with the Shadow practice.
- Alternate swings with the eyes open then closed.
- Feel swings focusing on your pivot and arm swing.
- Alternate two swings with the shadow and two swings hitting balls.

To Decrease Difficulty

- Practice Shadow Drill away from your ball-hitting station.

6. Distance Drill

It is important for you to be able to match how a swing feels with how far the golf ball travels. Ideally, you want to hit the ball as far as you can with consistent control. You can change either the speed of your swing or the club you select to achieve a specific, desired distance less than your maximum. As you are developing your swing, distance control may be inconsistent. However, this drill provides you with a system for measuring your progress as well as a distance assessment for each club.

Place 7 targets in a field at 10-yard intervals beginning at 90 yards away from the ball and ending at 160 yards away. Using a 5-iron, practice hitting balls toward the targets. Use an alignment club to determine your setup position for each swing. Determine the average distance you hit your 5-iron; most of your shots should cluster near the average. Continue this process with each club (woods and irons). You may need to adjust your yardage markers longer or shorter to fit your distance needs. This drill is best used with irons and woods on separate days.

Success Goal = consistent distance 50% or more of the time (this percentage will increase with practice). Record your distance on each of 10 swings using the 5-, 7-, 9-, and 3-irons and the 7-, 5-, and 3-woods. Record your scores in the spaces provided, and then calculate an average distance for each club.

Shot	Irons				Woods		
	5	7	9	3	7	5	3
1	——	——	——	——	——	——	——
2	——	——	——	——	——	——	——
3	——	——	——	——	——	——	——
4	——	——	——	——	——	——	——
5	——	——	——	——	——	——	——
6	——	——	——	——	——	——	——
7	——	——	——	——	——	——	——
8	——	——	——	——	——	——	——
9	——	——	——	——	——	——	——
10	——	——	——	——	——	——	——
Total	——	——	——	——	——	——	——
Average	——	——	——	——	——	——	——

Success Check
• Make practice swings to feel your swing pace ____

7. One-Leg Toe Drill

It is important to maintain your balance throughout your golf swing. Select any iron and take your regular full swing setup. Maintaining proper posture, place your rear foot directly behind your target-side foot. Place only the toe of your rear-side foot on the ground. Practice making swings using the 3-to-3 swing length from this position. Be sure to let your wrists cock, uncock, and recock. Notice how your body and hands feel. Be sure not to fall out of balance.

Success Goal = 30 total swings while staying in balance
10 swings, without ball ____
10 swings, ball on tee ____
10 swings, ball on ground ____

Success Check
• Pivot around your spine ____
• Butt of club to the target line ____

To Increase Difficulty
• Practice on the target leg only.

To Decrease Difficulty
• Rather than putting the rear foot directly behind the target foot, place it to the side, shoulder width apart.
• Alternate the regular swing motion between each 2 repetitions of the drill.

FULL SWING MOTION SUCCESS SUMMARY

You have been practicing your full swing and testing yourself by attaining each of the Step 3 Success Goals. You have no doubt experienced the distance versus accuracy dilemma that is part of the challenge of golf. Now ask someone trained in golf, your teacher, coach, or another trained observer to qualitatively evaluate your technique according to the checklist in Figure 3.2. Watch for good preparation (preswing routine, setup, grip, and posture), fluid swings, and weight transfer with a balanced follow-through. Each element of a good sequence should be checked as it is observed. Be sure to note the ball position differences with irons as compared to the ball position for woods.

You can swing as fast as you want, as long as you are in control and with balance. Davis Love III is one of the longest drivers on the PGA Tour. At one time in his career, he was the longest. He had an excessively long, full swing. Then, later, to become a better all-around player, rather than just the longest driver, he gave up some of his distance to become more accurate and more consistent. So if you hit the ball a long way and are rarely in the fairway, accuracy should be stressed. If you hit it straight, but need distance, then you need to develop a faster swing speed, and not worry if it's not quite as accurate, like Greg Norman. That extra 10 yards will be worth the slightly off-line shots that may or may not result.

STEP
4

GOLF BALL FEEDBACK: LEARNING FROM BALL FLIGHT

T he full swing motion is the foundation of your golf game. Like most sport skills the result of each shot tells the performer what happened with the swing. In basketball, the ball either goes through the hoop or is shot with too much or too little force or is off-target to the side. Similarly, in golf the flight of the ball gives you information about your swing. Both the direction the ball travels through the air and the distance attained are important. Say you hit a shot that goes 200 yards—the shot's distance is good, but if the ball lands 20 yards right of the target, the overall result may not be effective.

Why Is it Important to Learn From the Flight of Your Ball?

The flight of your golf ball is your "teacher" when you practice and play. Most of the fundamental swing errors of golfers at any level can be identified through understanding which errors cause particular ball flight patterns. Learning to observe and interpret your ball flight will allow more effective and efficient practice because you can self-correct and improve your swing fundamentals.

The best way to understand fundamental errors is to watch the ball flight after you hit each shot. If your golf ball goes in a straight line with only a slight curve to the right or left, you have a good start. If your ball lands too short or too far past the target, you probably are not swinging the club at the appropriate speed or you have selected the wrong club. If your ball flies in a straight line but goes to the left or right of the target, you have made what is called a *path error*. On the other hand, if your ball curves

excessively while in the air, your shot is referred to as either a *hook* or a *slice*, depending on the direction of the curve. These curving flight paths are the results of errors in the angle at which the face of the club strikes the ball. The possible combinations of ball flight paths and curvatures are illustrated in Figure 4.1.

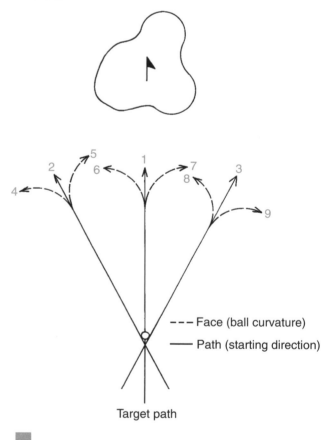

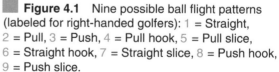

Figure 4.1 Nine possible ball flight patterns (labeled for right-handed golfers): 1 = Straight, 2 = Pull, 3 = Push, 4 = Pull hook, 5 = Pull slice, 6 = Straight hook, 7 = Straight slice, 8 = Push hook, 9 = Push slice.

It is important to train yourself to see the ball flight and remember what causes the characteristics you observe. Focus on a consistent swing first, striving for smoothness and speed. You can then learn to control the direction and angle of approach of the club to the ball. The faster the club is traveling when it squarely contacts the ball, the farther the ball goes. In fact, research has shown that a well-controlled speed of between 65 to 85 percent of your maximum swing speed is best for both speed and accuracy. So don't try to "kill" the ball; instead, swing at a fast, controlled rate (65 to 85 percent of your fastest swing).

How to Learn From the Flight of Your Ball

There are two important things to remember when trying to learn from the flight of your ball: (1) always aim at a specific target and (2) use a consistent setup position so that you start each swing in the same way.

Observe the flight of your ball to determine whether it starts out traveling in a straight line or curves in the air from the very beginning. If you are a right-handed golfer and your shot curves dramatically to the right, it is a slice; if it curves to the left, it is a hook. If you are left-handed, your slice goes to the left, your hook to the right. Hooks or slices result from the clubhead being at an angle when it meets the ball, thereby imparting spin to the ball. A slice is a result of an open clubface, and a hook is the result of a closed clubface (see Figure 4.1).

Sometimes a golf ball travels in a straight line but still lands off to the right or left of the target. If you were lined up straight at the target when you hit the ball but it went straight and landed off-target, it is probably because the club traveled in a path that aimed or pointed in that direction (see Figure 4.1). This is quite similar to a right-handed baseball batter who hits the ball over first base or pulls it over third base even though he or she is lined up aiming toward second base. When a right-handed golfer pushes the ball, it lands to the right of the target because the clubhead has been pushed in that direction during the swing. On the other hand, the ball is generally pulled across the normal target line when the ball travels in a straight line but lands to the left of the target. For a left-handed golfer, a ball traveling straight but landing to the left is a push, whereas one landing to the right of target is a pull.

The only thing that directly affects the flight of your ball is the way your club contacts it at impact. There are five club factors that affect the way energy is imparted from club to ball:

1. Clubhead speed at impact
2. Path on which the club is swung
3. Position of clubface at impact
4. Squareness of contact of clubface with the ball
5. Angle of approach of clubface

Each of these elements may be affected by your setup position in relation to the target.

Each club is a different length and has a different clubface angle. These two factors influence how fast the club moves when it contacts the ball and the angle of the force that is imparted. In addition, it is possible to control the trajectory of the ball flight by changing the angle at which the club is swung downward at the ball or changing the ball position. If you contact the ball above its *equator*, or centerline, it travels at a lower angle; if you contact the ball below its equator, the ball travels higher. That is why irons are designed to hit down through the ball and strike the ball below its center, whereas fairway woods typically are swung in such a way as to strike the ball just after the club reaches the lowest spot in its pendular swing. Note that your setup position for woods with the location of the ball to the target side of center also facilitates the flatter trajectory and results in longer distances. In contrast, the putter is designed to hit the ball squarely in its center and is swung in an essentially straight or horizontal line.

The golf swing is fundamentally a very simple pendular or arc motion. If you think of your arms and the club as a pendulum, the swing is a very understandable motion. The position and speed of the club when it contacts the ball determines how far the ball goes. The path on which the club swings determines the starting direction, whereas the angle of the face of the club determines the spin imparted to the ball. Because the club controls the ball and you control the club, you can become your own self-corrector by understanding the ball flight influences summarized in Figure 4.2.

FIGURE
4.2 **KEYS TO SUCCESS**

THE FLIGHT OF THE BALL
Greater distance is attained by

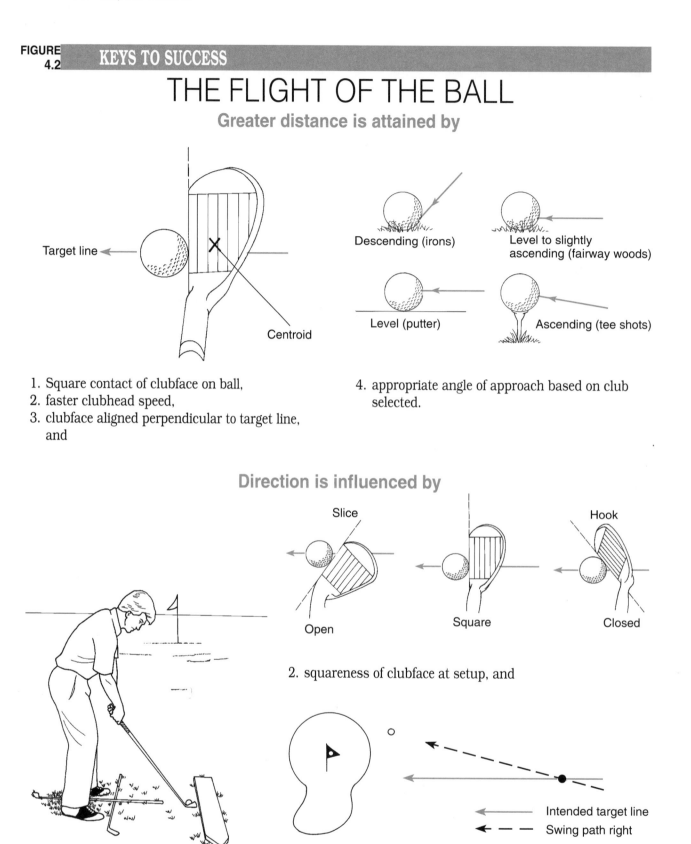

1. Square contact of clubface on ball,
2. faster clubhead speed,
3. clubface aligned perpendicular to target line, and

4. appropriate angle of approach based on club selected.

Direction is influenced by

1. Alignment to target at setup,
2. squareness of clubface at setup, and
3. swing path along target line at impact.

BALL FLIGHT FEEDBACK SUCCESS STOPPERS

There are two primary types of errors that can be observed in the flight of the ball: directional and distance errors. These can be summarized as follows:

1. The direction is primarily affected by

   ■ the aiming (alignment) of your body and the clubhead at setup,

   ■ the path through which you swing the club, and

   ■ the position of the clubface when it contacts the ball.

2. The distance the ball travels is primarily affected by

   ■ how squarely you hit the ball on the clubface,

   ■ how fast the club is traveling when it hits the ball, and

   ■ the club's angle of approach when it hits the ball.

The most fundamental problem causing errors in the direction of ball flight is poor alignment in the setup. In addition to this basic aiming problem, there may also be problems with the path of the club when you swing or with the angle of the clubface when it strikes the ball.

The way in which the clubface is aligned with the target line during the swing is another important factor. The angle of the clubface when it strikes the ball determines the ball's spin. Just like spin on a curveball in baseball, spin affects the way the golf ball travels through space. The face of the club should be square at contact (perpendicular to the target line). If it is open, a slice results; if closed, a hook.

To tell what happened when your ball lands off-target, ask yourself these two questions: (1) Did the ball travel straight toward the right or left of the target? If so, your error was probably a path or alignment error. (2) Did the ball curve excessively while in the air? If so, your error was likely a clubface error.

ERROR	CORRECTION
Direction: Path	
1. Ball travels straight but lands left or right of target. A path error due to an alignment problem.	1. Adjust alignment of body to square position. Stance should be parallel to target. Check feet, hips, and shoulders. **Explanation:** Directional errors are primarily caused by one of two problems: lack of square alignment or club swung on a path not aligned to target.
2. Ball lands right or left of target due to path on which you swing club.	2. Swing club on path to target. Check alignment and use club alignment to visualize desired path of ball flight. **Explanation:** Direction of ball flight is primarily the same as the direction in which you swing the clubhead.

ERROR	CORRECTION
Direction: Clubface	
1. Ball slices.	1. Allow clubhead to return to square at contact. Check to make sure hands are relaxed. Check release at contact. Check grip. **Explanation:** The angle of clubface in relation to the path of your swing determines sidespin imparted to the ball. An open clubface produces a slice.
2. Ball hooks.	2. Arms are stopping too soon and hands uncock early. Increase tension in hands slightly to change timing of release; be sure hands and arms start down as a unit. **Explanation:** Angle of clubface in relation to path of swing determines sidespin imparted to ball. A closed clubface produces a hook.
Distance	
1. Ball lands short of target, but flight looks about the right height.	1. Increase length of swing or swing speed. **Explanation:** Distance a golf ball travels depends on four things: the length of swing, speed of clubhead at moment of impact, squareness of contact made by club on ball, and angle of approach of the club to the ball.
2. Ball travels too high with an iron and lands short of target.	2. Angle of approach is too steep. Adjust angle of approach to be shallower or less steep by extending swing (making it wider on backswing and forwardswing; see explanation 5).
3. Ball seems to pop up in the air on the tee shot due to a steep approach.	3. Adjust angle of approach of club by extending swing (making it wider on backswing and forwardswing; see explanation 5). This flattens the angle into the ball.
4. Ball lands short of target, but swing seems about the right speed and length.	4. Check for square contact of clubface on ball. Club selection may need to be changed. **Explanation:** Each club has a *sweet spot* (also called a *centroid*), which is its center of mass extended to the clubface surface. This is the point on the clubface that can impart the most force to the ball, which can then travel its maximum distance. The farther away from the sweet spot the ball is hit, the more its distance and direction vary.

ERROR	CORRECTION
5. Ball shoots off sharply in front due to being hit in the hosel—a "shank." Upper body falls back on forwardswing.	5. Contact ball at sweet spot of club by keeping proper posture over ball on forwardswing.

BALL FLIGHT FEEDBACK

DRILLS

1. Long-Short Drill

To feel the effect the speed of the swing has on the distance a ball travels, experiment with slow and fast swing speeds. Using a good setup and your 5-, 7-, and 9-irons, hit three consecutive balls with the same club. Use a fast swing speed so the first shot goes long, a slow swing speed to make the second short, and a normal swing speed to make the third land in the middle. Practice changing the speed of your swing in order to adjust the distance.

Success Goal = hitting 9 balls, varying the speeds of the swings to make the balls travel long, short, then medium distance using these clubs:

a. 9-iron: long___ short___ medium___

b. 5- or 7-iron: long___ short___ medium___

c. Wood or long iron: long___ short___ medium___

Success Check

• Remember faster swings with control produce longer shots ____

To Increase Difficulty

• Use other clubs (e.g., 8-, 7-, 6-irons).

To Decrease Difficulty

• Focus on one club only; hit 9 balls with that club before changing to another.

2. Pop-Up Drill

The trajectory of a golf ball is affected by the angle of approach of the clubhead at contact. Using one club (a 5- or 7-iron), make your shots travel higher or lower by adjusting the angle of approach of your swing or by shifting the position of the ball in relation to the center of your stance.

Success Goal = hit 12 total balls, making them travel at different heights by adjusting the angle of approach

    a. 3 balls hit at steep angle ____

    b. 3 balls hit at shallow angle (flatter bottom on arc) ____

    c. 3 balls hit at normal angle ____

    d. 1 ball hit at steep angle ____

    e. 1 ball hit at shallow angle ____

Success Check

- Balls struck on a downward (steep) angle fly higher ____
- Moving ball back in stance produces higher ball flight ____

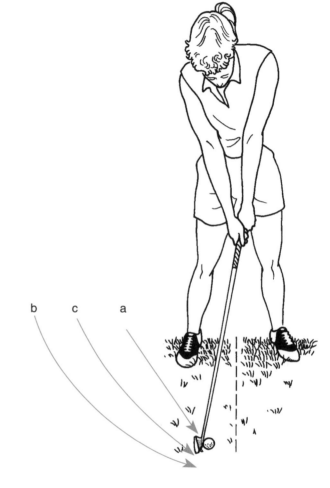

To Increase Difficulty

- Vary the angle with each swing.
- Use different clubs or produce the same angle of flight with different clubs.

To Decrease Difficulty

- Hit multiple shots with the same angle.

3. Slice and Hook Drill

Adjusting the angle of the clubface when it contacts the ball allows you to make the ball either hook or slice. For a hook, use a light grip pressure to cause the clubhead to be closed at contact. For a slice, increase tension in your hands and wrists, preventing the hands from releasing or the clubhead from returning to square. This lack of wrist action causes the clubhead to remain open at contact.

Be careful not to confuse the directional errors of a push or a pull with the intentional slices or hooks, which curve in flight.

Success Goal = hitting 28 total slices and hooks by adjusting angle at which clubface contacts ball

  a. Hit 5 slices ____

  b. Hit 5 hooks ____

  c. Hit 5 balls straight ____

  d. Hit 3 slices ____

  e. Hit 3 hooks ____

  f. Hit 3 straight ____

  g. Hit 1 slice ____

  h. Hit 1 straight ____

  i. Hit 1 hook ____

  j. Hit 1 straight ____

Slice position

Success Check

• Clubhead closed (light grip) produces a hook ____
• Clubhead open (tight grip) produces a slice ____

To Increase Difficulty

• Alternate slices and hooks with each swing.
• Use a variety of clubs.
• Attempt to vary the degree (severity) of the slice or hook.

To Decrease Difficulty

• Work on only slicing or hooking the ball.

4. Two-by-Four Drill

To check the swing path of your club, place a two-by-four piece of wood beyond the ball and parallel to the target line. Place your ball about 3 inches in from the board and hit it. (For safety reasons, be sure the board extends about 2 feet to the nontarget side of the ball, or substitute your golf bag for the board.)

Success Goal = hitting 15 total shots in a row (3 with each club) without touching the board during the swing

       3 shots, 5-iron ____   3 shots, 3-iron ____

       3 shots, 7-iron ____   3 shots, wood ____

       3 shots, 9-iron ____

Success Check

• Keep club path aligned with target _____

To Increase Difficulty

• Move board closer to ball.

To Decrease Difficulty

• Move board farther away from ball.

• Use a club lying on the ground rather than the 2-by-4.

5. Simon Says: Systematic Ball Manipulation Drill

Understanding how to manipulate the flight of a golf ball is the most important step in becoming a proficient golfer. In order to test your ability to control your swing, attempt to repeat each of the following characteristics.

Success Goal

On command, produce each of the following types of shots. Attempt each shot five times:

  a. Push _____

  b. Pull _____

  c. Slice _____

  d. Hook _____

  e. Top the ball _____

  f. Hit ball at very bottom (pop it up) _____

  g. Hit ball off toe of club _____

  h. Hit ball off heel of club ("shank") _____

  i. Swing club very fast and hit ball far _____

  j. Swing club very slowly and hit ball square, straight, and not very far _____

  k. Hit ball as perfectly as possible _____

Success Check

• Review ball flight laws _____

To Increase Difficulty

• Use different club for each shot.

• Vary the type of shot each time.

To Decrease Difficulty

• Focus on either directional or height changes.

6. Bogey Challenge Drill

With a partner, take turns playing follow-the-leader. If your partner calls for or designates a slice and then successfully hits one, you must also hit a slice. If you fail, you receive the next letter in the word "bogey" (or another golf-related word of your choice), as in the basketball game of Horse. Each time you miss a called shot, you receive another letter in the word. The loser is the first person to have the entire word (to have missed 5 called shots).

Success Goal = to avoid acquiring all letters in the word *bogey* by successfully hitting all shots your partner expects you to execute; to attempt to call and hit shots that your partner cannot execute

Penalty letters   *spell:* ___ ___ ___ ___ ___

(B)   (o)   (g)   (e)   (y)

Success Check

• Consider the ball flight "rules" to produce the desired flights ___

To Increase Difficulty

• Use a shorter word (e.g., "par").

To Decrease Difficulty

• Allow each golfer 2 or 3 attempts to produce the desired shot.

BALL FLIGHT FEEDBACK SUCCESS SUMMARY

Effective golfers are able to control the flight of their golf ball and learn from it if errors occur. By experimenting with the ball flight "laws" you will be able to execute desired shots, and learn to analyze your own problems and correct them. Experiment with the principles described in Figure 4.2, and use a partner or experienced teacher or friend to challenge you to be able to execute desired shots on demand (review Drills 5 and 6). As you practice and play, notice the trade-off between distance and accuracy, but remember to focus on matching the feel of the full swing with the shot results.

STEP
5

PITCH SHOTS: APPROACHING THE GREEN

Ever wonder how pros shoot those low scores? In addition to lots of practice they learn to get their pitch shots close to the hole. Most people think pros hit all the greens in regulation. Wrong! If that's your dream, dream on—but keep practicing in the reality that pitching is key to shooting low scores.

Pitching is perhaps the shot used most frequently, next to teeing off and putting. You begin the pitch shot when your full swing with a 9-iron goes too far. The actual distance will vary with each golfer but generally ranges between 80 and 20 yards. The pitch shot differs in purpose from the full swing in that accuracy is the major goal, not distance.

Why Is Pitching Important?

The pitch shot has a high trajectory and rolls very little when it lands on the green. This makes it a desirable shot to use near the green because it tends to stay on the green rather than roll off. The pitch shot is a very versatile shot usually used about 10 to 90 yards from the green, depending on your skill level. This shot provides the most variation in distance control of all the shots in golf.

How to Execute the Pitch Shot

The pitch shot uses the setup position and swing motion of the full swing with irons discussed in Steps 2 and 3, but with two differences: The swing length is reduced, and the stance is narrower (see Figure 5.1). The pitch shot uses a 3-to-3 or 4-to-4 swing length, rather than a 5-to-5 full swing motion. This reduced swing motion provides greater control of direction and distance. A stance slightly narrower than shoulder width helps you develop a swing for control rather than distance. The clubs used for the pitch shot are the 9-iron, pitching wedge (PW), and the sand wedge (SW). A loft wedge is sometimes used by professionals and advanced players.

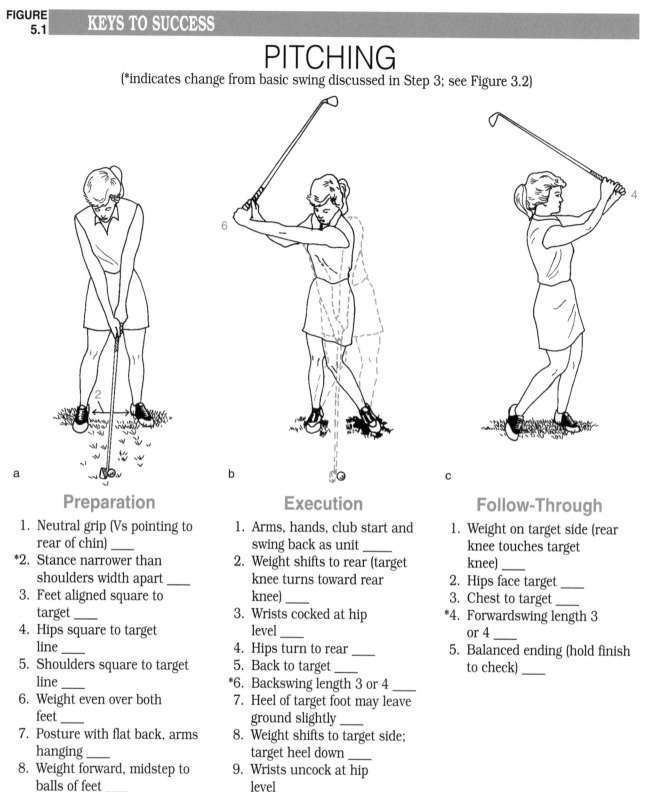

FIGURE 5.1

KEYS TO SUCCESS

PITCHING
(*indicates change from basic swing discussed in Step 3; see Figure 3.2)

Preparation

1. Neutral grip (Vs pointing to rear of chin) ___
*2. Stance narrower than shoulders width apart ___
3. Feet aligned square to target ___
4. Hips square to target line ___
5. Shoulders square to target line ___
6. Weight even over both feet ___
7. Posture with flat back, arms hanging ___
8. Weight forward, midstep to balls of feet ___
9. Ball position center ___
10. Square blade (blade perpendicular to target line)

Execution

1. Arms, hands, club start and swing back as unit ___
2. Weight shifts to rear (target knee turns toward rear knee) ___
3. Wrists cocked at hip level ___
4. Hips turn to rear ___
5. Back to target ___
*6. Backswing length 3 or 4 ___
7. Heel of target foot may leave ground slightly ___
8. Weight shifts to target side; target heel down ___
9. Wrists uncock at hip level ___
10. Hips return to square ___
11. Arms, hands, club extended at contact with ball ___
12. Wrists recocked at target-side hip level ___
13. Hips turning to target ___

Follow-Through

1. Weight on target side (rear knee touches target knee) ___
2. Hips face target ___
3. Chest to target ___
*4. Forwardswing length 3 or 4 ___
5. Balanced ending (hold finish to check) ___

PITCHING SUCCESS STOPPERS

The same ball flight errors that apply to the full swing apply to pitching. These should be reviewed (see Step 4). The errors listed below are the most common ones seen in pitching.

ERROR	CORRECTION
1. You hit the ball on its top, giving inadequate loft in trajectory.	1. Remember that the 9-iron, PW, and SW are the shortest clubs; you may be standing up too straight during the execution phase. Maintain proper body posture from setup through complete swing.
2. You hit the ball too long or too short of target.	2. The club used, swing length, and swing speed determine distance of ball flight. Practice hitting balls with swing lengths of 3-to-3 and 4-to-4 (not 5-to-5) with your 9-iron, PW, and SW. Note distances ball travels.
3. You hit the ball in hosel of club.	3. a. Check ball position in setup; may be too far toward your target foot, or too close to the rear foot, rather than in center of stance. b. You may be moving your body forward on forwardswing. Practice the One-Leg Drill from Step 3.
4. Ball flight has low trajectory.	4. a. Check ball position; it may be too far back (to rear of stance) rather than in center. b. Practice Cocking Drill from Step 3.
5. You hit the ground behind ball.	5. a. Maintain posture from setup position through complete swing (see correction 3). b. Allow arm swing and hand action to be continuous on forwardswing through completion of swing, matching backswing length.

PITCHING

DRILLS

1. Tee-Down Without a Ball Drill

The Tee-Down Drill will help you feel the arm swing and hand action of the pitch shot. Place a tee in the hole in the end of your golf club grip. Practice taking normal swings of 3-to-3 swing length. With proper wrist cocking, the tee should point to the ground on the backswing (at position 3) and on the forwardswing (at 3).

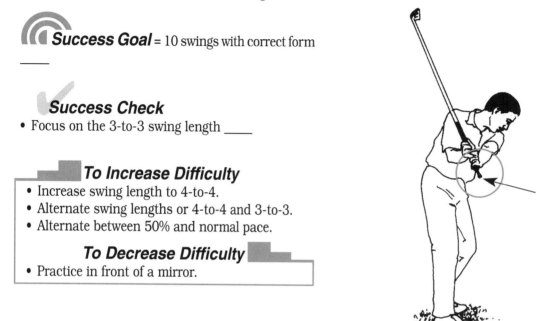

Tee

Success Goal = 10 swings with correct form _____

Success Check
• Focus on the 3-to-3 swing length _____

To Increase Difficulty
• Increase swing length to 4-to-4.
• Alternate swing lengths or 4-to-4 and 3-to-3.
• Alternate between 50% and normal pace.

To Decrease Difficulty
• Practice in front of a mirror.

2. Tee-Down Drill with a Ball

With a PW, SW, or 9-iron with a tee in the grip end (as in Drill 1), hit balls toward targets at 20 and 40 yards. Check for tee-down position at backswing and forwardswing.

Success Goal = 60 total swings with correct form and balls landing within 15 feet of target
a. 20 total swings with one club
   10 at 40-yard target _____
   5 full swing practice swings _____
   10 at 20-yard target _____
b. Repeat (a) with a different club
   10 at 40-yard target _____
   5 full swing practice swings _____
   10 at 20-yard target _____
c. Hit 20 shots, changing clubs and targets each time _____

Success Check
• Focus on swing length _____
• Hold finish to check length with distance _____

To Increase Difficulty
• Decrease desired landing radius to 10 feet.
• Increase shot distance to 50 and 60 yards.
• Add accuracy element to success goal (50% of shots land within 15 feet of target).

To Decrease Difficulty
• Increase desired landing radius to 20 feet.
• Hit balls from a tee just above the ground.
• Practice with 1 club of your choice.

3. Alternate Swing Length Drill

To determine the swing length and club you need for different distances using the pitch shot, place targets at 10-yard intervals from 40 through 90 yards. Practice hitting 10 balls to each target using 3-to-3 and 4-to-4 swing lengths. Take four full swing practice swings between each 10 shots. The appropriate club and swing length for a given distance should allow you to hit balls within 10 yards or your target 50% or more of the time.

Record the average distance you hit the balls with a 3-to-3 swing length using a SW, a PW, and a 9-iron. Then switch to a 4-to-4 swing length and record the average distance hit with a SW, a PW, and a 9-iron.

Success Goal = 60 total swings

Shot	3-to-3 swing length			4-to-4 swing length		
	SW	PW	9-iron	SW	PW	9-iron
1	____	____	____	____	____	____
2	____	____	____	____	____	____
3	____	____	____	____	____	____
4	____	____	____	____	____	____
5	____	____	____	____	____	____
6	____	____	____	____	____	____
7	____	____	____	____	____	____
8	____	____	____	____	____	____
9	____	____	____	____	____	____
10	____	____	____	____	____	____
Total	____	____	____	____	____	____
Average	____	____	____	____	____	____

Success Check

• Hold finish ____
• Match distance with swing length and feel ____

To Increase Difficulty

• Vary swing pace from normal to 50% or normal.
• Hit balls with eyes closed, using a tee.
• Decrease target radius to 10 feet.

To Decrease Difficulty

• Use tees.
• Select club of your choice.
• Reduce number of swings to 30.

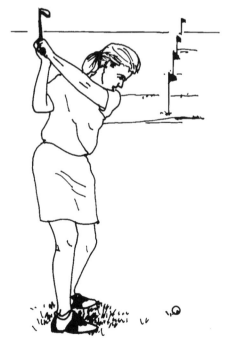

4. Variable Loft Drill

Using a single club (either 9-iron, PW, or SW), vary the position of the ball in relation to your stance: off the target heel, off the rear heel, and center. Note the changes in ball flight trajectory ranging from low to high achieved without changes in your swing but merely with changes in the positions of the balls.

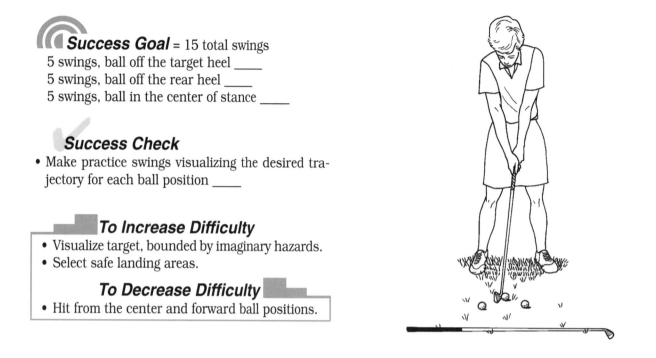

Success Goal = 15 total swings

5 swings, ball off the target heel ____
5 swings, ball off the rear heel ____
5 swings, ball in the center of stance ____

Success Check

• Make practice swings visualizing the desired trajectory for each ball position ____

To Increase Difficulty

• Visualize target, bounded by imaginary hazards.
• Select safe landing areas.

To Decrease Difficulty

• Hit from the center and forward ball positions.

PITCHING SUCCESS SUMMARY

Pitching is a fun shot and provides a good practice for your full swing—the only differences are a shorter swing length and narrower stance. No players hit all the greens in regulation all the time, so plan ahead and put in time practicing the drills provided for the pitch shot. You will be amazed at how often you use this shot as you have the opportunity to play more golf. Be sure to have a friend, professional, or practice partner check your techniques using the checklist in Figure 5.1.

STEP 6

CHIP SHOTS: SCORING WITH YOUR SHORT GAME

To pitch or chip is a dilemma all golfers face on the course—and so will you. The pitch shot, as you practiced in Step 5, is a high-trajectory shot with little roll, while the chip shot is a low-trajectory shot with lots of roll. The specific situation you face on the course and your relative proficiency for a chip or pitch will determine which shot is the right decision.

The chip shot is a shorter and more controlled motion than the pitch shot. The 7- and 9-irons will be used when practicing the chip shot. After you become proficient with the 7- and 9-irons, the chip shot technique can be used with all clubs.

Why Is Chipping Important?

The purpose of the chip shot is to land the ball on the green and have it roll toward the hole. There are many situations around the green when you want to control the flight of the ball to have it land on the green and roll toward the pin. Figure 6.1 illustrates two common situations in which your ball lands near the green and you use the chip shot:

1. Your ball lands near, but not on, the green; or

2. Your ball lands near the green, but with sand or water between you and the green.

Note that the only difference between the two situations is that there is a sand bunker present in one illustration. This sand bunker should not be viewed as some insurmountable obstacle.

Using the practice drills that follow, you will be able to determine distance from the green you are comfortable using the chip shot, and you will learn to control and visualize the ball trajectory of various length chip shots. Figure 6.1 shows two golf holes where pitching or chipping are likely to occur. Once

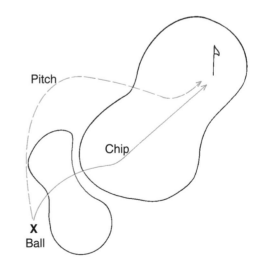

a

b

Figure 6.1 Two golf holes for chipping or pitching.

you practice different distances and trajectories, it will transfer to the course, allowing you to select the chip or pitch shot for the situation around the green.

On the course whenever you have a choice between a pitch shot and a chip shot, and you feel equally comfortable with each, select the chip shot as long as there is room for the ball to land on the green and roll to the pin. The chip shot is easier to control due to the shorter swing length and less body movement it requires.

How to Execute the Chip Shot

The swing motion of the chip shot uses only a 1-to-1 or 2-to-2 swing length, depending upon the distance required. The shoulders, arms, hands, and club move as a unit, with no wrist motion. The swinging motion is a pendular motion, which is smooth and continuous.

The setup position is important in achieving the desired low trajectory. This position differs from the pitch shot and the full swing in the following ways: Your feet are placed narrower than your shoulders, with the alignment of your feet and hips slightly open. To open your stance, move your target-side foot back about 4 inches off of the target line. This makes your lower body turn slightly toward the target, which helps to reduce your lower-body motion on the backswing. Be sure your shoulders remain square or parallel to the target line.

Your upper body leans toward the target, placing your weight more on the target side. Note that your arms and hands are just inside your target leg, which delofts, or decreases, the natural loft of the clubface (see Figure 6.2). The palm of your rear hand will face the ground. The rear hand wrist is bent and the target wrist is straight. Your arms and shoulders create an isosceles triangle (i.e., both arms extended) that is maintained *throughout* the swing motion. Your head and swing center are on the target side of the ball. In this position you see more of the target side

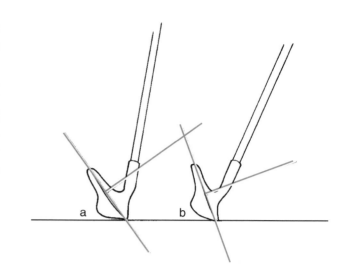

Figure 6.2   Two clubs showing (a) natural loft and (b) delofted.

of the ball rather than looking straight down onto the top of the ball as in the pitch shot and full swing setups.

The 7-iron and the 9-iron are suggested for the chip shot during your initial practice and play. On the golf course, your club selection for the chip shot depends on the distance the ball is from the pin and the amount of green between the ball and the pin. The amount of trajectory and roll varies between these two clubs. The 9-iron creates a higher trajectory than the 7-iron and has less roll. The rule of thumb to use as you play is to select the 9-iron for a chip shot when the distance from the ball to the pin is 10 yards or less, or there is 10 yards or less of green to the pin. Select the 7-iron for longer shots when there is greater than 10 yards of green to the pin. Begin practicing with other clubs (e.g., 6-,8-, PW, or SW) when, during actual play on the course, you can successfully chip the ball within 3 feet of the pin 7 out of 10 times using the 7- or 9-iron. Too many club choices can be confusing. Keep your club choices to a minimum for best results as you are learning the game. The Keys to Success for executing the chip shot are shown in Figure 6.3.

FIGURE 6.3 **KEYS TO SUCCESS**

CHIPPING
(*indicates change from the basic full swing technique)

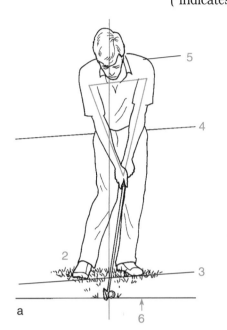
a

b

c

Preparation

1. Neutral grip (V's pointing to rear of chin)
   *Rear wrist bent ___
   *Target wrist straight ___
*2. Stance narrower than shoulder width ___
*3. Feet aligned open to target line ___
*4. Hips aligned open relative to target line ___
5. Shoulders aligned square relative to target line ___
*6. Weight on target side
   Head to target side of ball ___
   Swing center to target side of ball ___
   Hands to target side of ball ___
7. Posture over ball, with flat back ___
8. Weight forward, midstep to balls of feet ___
9. Center ball position___
*10. Square blade, *delofted ___

Execution

*1. Shoulders, arms, hands, club start as unit ___
*2. No weight shift on backswing ___
*3. No wrist cock
   *Rear wrist bent ___
   *Target wrist straight ___
4. Hips turn to rear ___
5. Half-turn back (back to target) ___
*6. Backswing length 1 or 2 ___
*7. No weight shift on forwardswing ___
*8. Shoulders, arms, hands, club move as unit ___
*9. Maintain unitary arm action ___
*10. Unit at contact ___
*11. Hips turn halfway to target ___

Follow-Through

1. Weight on target side (rear knee touches target knee) ___
2. Hips face target ___
*3. Half-turn of chest ___
*4. Forwardswing length equals backswing (1 or 2) ___
*5. Blade square in relation to target line ___
6. Hold end position to check for balance ___
7. Wrist position
   *Rear wrist bent ___
   *Target wrist straight ___

CHIP SHOT SUCCESS STOPPERS

Learning to execute a chip shot is easier if you understand how it is different from the full swing and pitch shot. Ball flight errors are the result of your setup and swing, and, therefore, are common to all swings, including the chip shot. It helps if you can see or imagine the common errors. The most common chip shot errors are listed below, along with suggestions on how to correct them.

ERROR	CORRECTION
1. Hitting the ball on its top resulting in no loft.	1. Notice if your wrists are bent on the follow-through. Instead, your hands, wrists, and arms should work as a unit throughout swing with rear wrist bend and target wrist straight. Practice the Extended Club Drill (# 4). Hold follow-through to check position.
2. Ball consistently goes too far beyond target.	2. a. Compare forwardswing lengths with distances the ball travels. b. Practice Ladder Drill (# 5) to develop feel for distance the ball travels.
3. You hit ground behind the ball, causing ball to go too short a distance.	3. Maintain proper posture with weight on target side; swing as unit throughout swing (see Figure 6.3a-c).
4. Chip shot with 7-iron has excessively high trajectory.	4. a. Check setup position, with arms, hands, and club in straight line, with club slightly delofted (see Fig 6.3a). b. Maintain position by keeping hands in front of ball through-out swing.
5. Ball consistently goes off-target.	5. a. Check setup alignment of body and club. b. Practice Parallel Club Drill (#2) noting target alignment and resulting shot direction. c. Practice alignment and swing without parallel clubs.

CHIPPING

DRILLS

1. Elephant Trunk Drill

The chip shot is characterized by hands that are inactive. The shoulders, arms, hands, and club work as a unit, both straight back and straight through.

Without a club, take your setup position. Let your arms hang freely. Place your palms together, creating a praying hands or elephant trunk position. Point your fingers to the rear side. Maintain extended arms while swinging them back and forth in a pendular motion (1-to-1 and 2-to-2 swing lengths). Keep your fingers to the rear throughout the swing (see Figures a-c).

Success Goal = 10 repetitions with fluid motion

    Five 1-to-1 swing lengths _____
    Five 2-to-2 swing lengths _____

To Increase Difficulty

• Alternate moving your wrist on the backswing (undesired) with not using the wrists (desired) to feel difference.

Success Check

• Back—through—hold _____
• Equal back—equal through _____

a

b   c

2. Parallel Clubs Without a Ball Drill

Consistency in your alignment is important in developing a repeatable chip shot. Alignment and swing motion can be practiced together by placing two clubs on the ground, parallel to each other and apart just a little more than the width of the clubhead. Direct the clubs toward the target.

Using a 7- or 9-iron, take your setup position with your club between the parallel clubs and square to the target. Using a pendular motion, swing the club back and forth. Maintain the square blade position as you swing the club in the track.

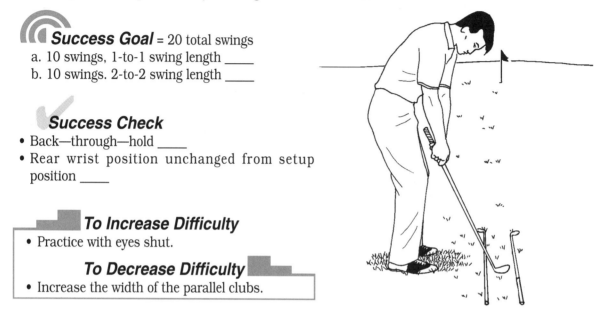

Success Goal = 20 total swings
a. 10 swings, 1-to-1 swing length ____
b. 10 swings. 2-to-2 swing length ____

Success Check
• Back—through—hold ____
• Rear wrist position unchanged from setup position ____

To Increase Difficulty
• Practice with eyes shut.

To Decrease Difficulty
• Increase the width of the parallel clubs.

3. Parallel Clubs With a Ball Drill

Using parallel clubs from the previous drill as a guide, hit balls from between them and toward a target about 15 feet away. Alternate 1-to-1 and 2-to-2 swing lengths. Maintain the same swing pace for both swing lengths. Note the differences in distance and height of the ball flight from varying the length of the swing. Check that every ball hit with a 2-to-2 swing length goes farther than those hit with a 1-to-1 swing length. (Note that hips and shoulders are open.)

Success Goal = 8 total pendular swings using 1-to-1 and 2-to-2 swing lengths, alternating with and without parallel clubs (2-to-2 shots longer than 1-to-1)
a. 2 swings, 1-to-1 swing length with clubs ____
2 swings, 2-to-2 swing length with clubs ____
2-to-2 shots longer than 1-to-1 ____
b. 1 swing, 1-to-1 swing length without clubs ____
1 swing, 2-to-2 swing length without clubs ____
2-to-2 shots longer than 1-to-1 ____
c. 1 swing, 1-to-1 swing length with clubs ____
1 swing, 2-to-2 swing length without clubs ____
2-to-2 shot longer than 1-to-1 ____

Success Check
- Feel your arms and shoulders as a unit ____
- Back, through, hold ____
- Square blade back and through ____
- Rear wrist bent on finish ____

To Increase Difficulty
- Swing with eyes closed.
- Alternate targets without parallel clubs.

To Decrease Difficulty
- Use only one club, a 7- or 9-iron.

4. Extended Club Drill

Active hands can be the source of both distance and directional errors in the chip shot. Often your hands are active, but you may not be consciously aware of their movement. This drill helps you feel whether your hands are too active.

Using a 9-iron, take your setup position. Add a second club, as in Figure a, making an extension to your 9-iron. Take practice swings using the 1-to-1 and 2-to-2 swing lengths (see Figures b and c). If your hands are too active, the clubface will pass your hands at impact, and the second shaft will hit you in the side, as shown in Figure d below.

Success Goal = 8 total extended club swings
- 4 swings, 1-to-1 swing length ____
- 4 swings, 2-to-2 swing length ____

Success Check
- Maintain the rear hand setup position ____
- Feel the arm and shoulder unit ____
- Hold finish, check position ____

To Increase Difficulty
- Hit balls with the extended club.
- Hit balls with the extended club to different target lengths.

To Decrease Difficulty
- Reduce swings to 4.
- Practice only one swing length, your choice.

a　　　b　　　c　　　d

——————————————— Desired ———————————————　ERROR: Hands too active

5. Ladder Drill

The 7- and 9-iron chip shots vary in trajectory and amount of roll. This drill helps you experiment with the amount of swing pace and swing length required to hit the balls different distances in the air.

Place a series of clubs on the ground to serve as targets 10, 20, 30, and 40 feet away. Number the clubs from 1 (nearest) to 4. Using 1-to-1 and 2-to-2 swing lengths, practice hitting balls different distances using a single club. Then practice achieving different distances with another club. Each ball should land between the two targets you've selected as short and long boundaries for that shot.

Success Goal = 20 total shots using 7- and 9-irons

7-iron:

        2 shots, 1-to-1 swing length, landing between targets 1 and 2 _____

        2 shots, 2-to-2 swing length, landing between targets 3 and 4 _____

        2 shots, 1-to-1 swing length, landing between targets 2 and 3 _____

9-iron:

        2 shots, 1-to-1 swing length, landing between targets 1 and 2 _____

        2 shots, 2-to-2 swing length, landing between targets 3 and 4 _____

        2 shots, 1-to-1 swing length, landing between targets 2 and 3 _____

7-iron:

        2 shots, 1-to-1 swing length, landing between targets 2 and 3 _____

        2 shots, 2-to-2 swing length, landing between targets 3 and 4 _____

9-iron:

        2 shots, 1-to-1 swing length, landing between targets 2 and 3 _____

        2 shots, 2-to-2 swing length, landing between targets 3 and 4 _____

Success Check

• Match feel of swing with result _____
• Hold finish until the ball stops _____

To Increase Difficulty

• Use only one shot per swing length.
• Reduce target radius to 5 feet.

To Decrease Difficulty

• Use only a 9-iron.
• Increase landing radius to 15 feet .

6. Obstacle Drill

The chip shot is often used on the course when a trap is between the ball and the pin (see Figure 6.1). Practicing the chip shot over obstacles helps you learn to focus on the chip motion rather than the obstacle.

Place your golf bag about 8 yards in front of your ball. Practice chipping over the bag toward targets 15, 20, and 25 yards away. Determine the appropriate club and swing length to have each ball stop within 10 feet of the desired target.

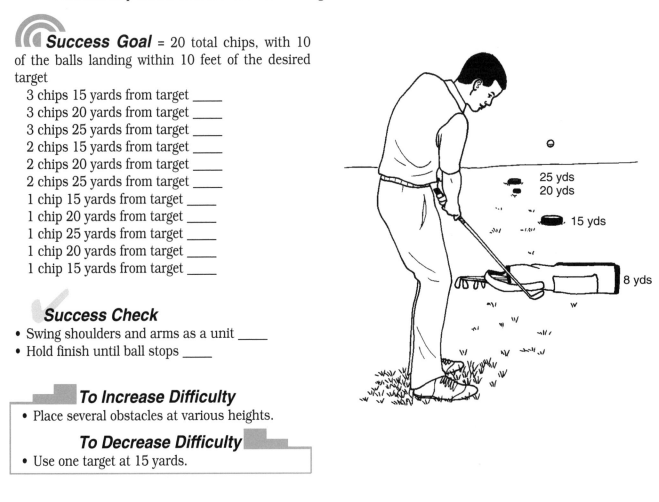

Success Goal = 20 total chips, with 10 of the balls landing within 10 feet of the desired target

3 chips 15 yards from target ____
3 chips 20 yards from target ____
3 chips 25 yards from target ____
2 chips 15 yards from target ____
2 chips 20 yards from target ____
2 chips 25 yards from target ____
1 chip 15 yards from target ____
1 chip 20 yards from target ____
1 chip 25 yards from target ____
1 chip 20 yards from target ____
1 chip 15 yards from target ____

Success Check

• Swing shoulders and arms as a unit ____
• Hold finish until ball stops ____

To Increase Difficulty

• Place several obstacles at various heights.

To Decrease Difficulty

• Use one target at 15 yards.

CHIP SHOT SUCCESS SUMMARY

When possible, spend time watching the pros and good amateurs as they play. Note the distances and situations around the green when they use the chip and pitch shots. Good players want control just like you. Keep track of your "up and downs" when you play. Remember the chip shot is a stroke-saving shot.

The chip shot technique can be developed quite quickly because it is shorter and more controlled than the pitch or full swing. You can become a good self-corrector as you use this checklist on yourself. Also, ask your playing partner, teacher, or another trained observer to qualitatively evaluate your technique according to the checklist in Figure 6.3. Each characteristic should be checked as it appears.

PUTTING: READING, ROLLING, AND RECORDING

There are three components to putting—the putting stroke, distance control, and being able to read greens. The putting stroke is used primarily on the greens. It differs from the other strokes you have learned in that the ball is rolled across the green rather than being hit into the air. This makes for greater stroke control and precision. As the ball rolls, the contour of the green affects ball direction and speed. Reading greens means learning to predict the influence of the green's contour on the roll of the putt.

Players often attribute the difference in their scores from one day to the next to their putting. Some days the four- and five-foot putts go in and other days they "just miss." Outside factors affect your ability to make putts that are not evident in your other strokes. The ball rolls on the ground and is affected by the (1) speed of greens which vary from one day to the next, (2) the different slope influences from flat to severely contoured, as well as (3) the putting surface which changes from smooth to very rough and bumpy with the amount of play the course gets. Playing early in the morning presents a very different surface from in the late afternoon, when cleat marks and dryness are more prominent.

Even with the changing conditions, putting is the easiest stroke to learn and exciting because it brings closure to each hole. To become a good putter you need to learn the basic putting stroke and how to control the distance the ball rolls. In addition, you must learn to read the greens and understand how the contour affects the ball as it rolls. The basic stroke is the most important factor. You can learn to read greens, but if the stroke is inconsistent, it won't help you.

Rules Specific to Putting

Lifting and Cleaning your Ball. On the putting green, you are allowed to lift the ball and clean it if you desire. This is not permitted until your ball is on the green. If you wish to clean your ball, you are required to "mark it" first and then lift it. This is also true if your ball is in the way of another golfer or might interfere with their line of putt. Under the USGA Rules (i.e., Rule #20.1), you are allowed to mark your ball by placing a small coin or ball marker just behind it, then lifting the ball to clean it. The ball *may not* be touched until the marker is placed behind the ball. When it is your turn to play, the ball must be replaced to the original position first, then pick up your marker.

Hitting a Ball or Flag on the Green. When putting from the green, you must not hit the flag or another golfer's ball. It is your responsibility to have the flag tended and moved aside. Also it is up to you to have an opponent "mark" his or her ball if it is in the way of your putt. If you happen to hit another ball, you must take a 2-stroke penalty and play your ball from where it comes to rest. An opponent's ball that has been moved must be replaced to its original position (USGA Rule #17.3).

Why Is Putting Important?

In an 18-hole round of golf, 50% of the strokes allotted toward par are for putting. This is a major indication of the role putting plays in the game. Anyone can become a good putter because strength is not a factor and, therefore, does not limit your ability. With practice you can develop a good putting stroke and begin to lower your scores while the other phases of your game are also improving.

How to Execute the Putting Stroke

The club used in executing the putting stroke is a putter. The putter differs greatly from the other clubs in its design. The clubface is almost vertical compared to the angled clubfaces of the other clubs. The putter is shorter than other clubs, and it has a more upright shaft.

The differences in the purpose of the stroke (to roll the ball) and the design of the club (shorter) require a modification in the setup position from other strokes. Start your putting setup position by gripping the club more in the palms of your hands rather than in the fingers (as in the full swing grip) (see Figure 7.1). Place the putter face behind the ball square to the desire target, with the bottom of the

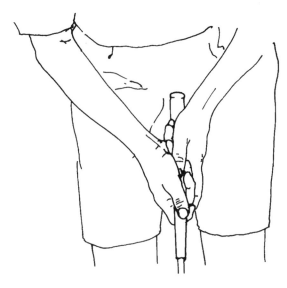

Figure 7.1 The putting grip is more in the palms of the hands.

club flat on the ground. Assume a correct posture position with your eyes directly over the ball or slightly behind the ball on the target line, your arms hanging from your shoulders, with the hands positioned under the shoulders (see Figure 7.2). Your weight should be evenly distributed across a square alignment. The ball should be positioned slightly to the target side of center (see Figure 7.3a).

Figure 7.2 When putting, your eyes should be directly over the ball and your hands under your shoulders.

The putting stroke motion is pendular. The club, hands, arms, and shoulders work as a unit (see Figures 7.3b and 7.3c). The upper and lower body are still, but not rigid, during the stroke. The length of the back- and forwardswings are equal. The stroke length is measured in inches and varies with the length of the putt. For example, 2 to 4 inches equals a 1-to-1 putting length. The stroke is smooth and continuous, back and then through the ball.

FIGURE 7.3   **KEYS TO SUCCESS**

PUTTING

(*indicates difference from basic full swing motion)

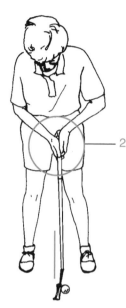  

a   b   c

Preparation

1. Read green and select target ___
*2. Grip in palms ___ (V's in grip point to respective shoulders)
3. Feet shoulder width apart ___
4. Weight evenly distributed on both feet ___
5. Weight forward, midstep to balls of feet___
6. Feet alignment square to putt line ___
7. Hips square to putt line ___
8. Shoulders square to target line ___
9. Posture with flat back ___
10. Eyes over ball ___
11. Ball position target side of center ___
12. Blade of club square to putt line ___

Execution

*1. Shoulders, arms, hands, putter swing back as unit ___
*2. Arms bent at elbows ___
*3. No weight shift on backswing ___
*4. No wrist cock ___
*5. Hips still on backswing ___
*6. Shoulders still on backswing ___
*7. Swing length 1, 2, or 3 ___
*8. No weight shift on forwardswing ___
*9. Shoulders, arms, hands, putter start as unit ___
*10. No wrist movement on forwardswing ___
*11. Shoulders, arms, hands, putter are unit at contact with ball ___
*12. Hips still on forward-swing ___
*13. Blade stays on target line ___

Follow-Through

1. Swing continues smoothly ___
*2. Shoulders, arms, hands, putter continue as unit ___
*3. Hips same position as setup ___
*4. Swing length 1, 2, or 3 ___
5. Hold position at end to check for balance ___
6. Square blade at end ___
7. Holds for a moment to check squareness ___
8. Swing length equal on both sides ___ (length of follow-through = length of backswing)

Distance Control

The pendular stroke allows for consistency as well as distance control. The length and pace of the stroke determine distance. For example, if you have a putt of three feet, make a short stroke with a slow pace. The converse is true for a putt of 30 feet. The stroke is longer with a faster pace.

Distance control is learned through trial and error just as throwing a ball. The key is to develop a consistent technique first. Then it is easier to adapt the stroke for various distances. The drills provided will give you a systematic approach to feeling distance.

Green Reading

Once you have developed a consistent putting stroke and distance control, learning to read the greens is your next objective. Greens vary in contour from very flat to very wavy. The wavy effects of a green are called undulations or slopes. A slope on the green has its greatest effect on the direction of the ball as the roll begins to slow down. With less speed, the ball is less able to resist the pull of gravity, so it curves more downhill.

Imagine a clock face, as illustrated in Figure 7.4. The hole is in the middle of the face. The high point of the slope is 12 and the low point is 6; the middle points of the slope are at 3 and 9. If you putted balls from each of the points around the clock face to the hole, the lines drawn on the face illustrate the ball curvature you could expect. Note that balls putted directly uphill from 6 and directly downhill from 12 are relatively straight. From each of the other points, as the ball slows down, it curves down the slope.

To apply the clock analogy to reading greens, move to a position about 10 feet directly behind your ball in line with the hole. Bend down or kneel (see Figure 7.5) in order to effectively see the slope of the green, specifically the slope closest to the hole. If there are no slopes, align the blade directly with the middle of the hole for a straight putt. If there is a slope, determine the high and the low points of the slope (i.e., 12 and 6 on the clock face) and where your ball is relative to those points. Visualize the ball rolling up or down the slope and curving into the hole. Pick a spot a few inches on the high side of the hole. Align your blade to that spot. As the ball rolls to the spot and slows down, it will curve toward the hole.

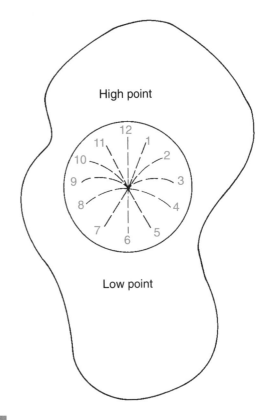

Figure 7.4 Ball curvature of a putted ball on a slope.

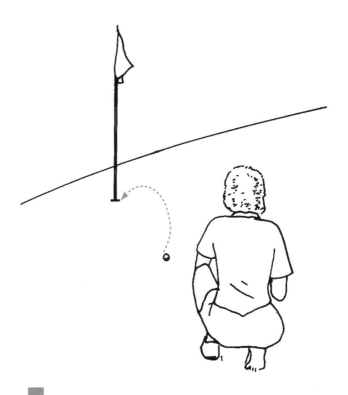

Figure 7.5 Bend down about 10 feet from the ball to see the slope of the green.

You can use the name of the ball—Wilson, Ultra, Top Flight, etc.—to align your blade more accurately. Place the name lengthwise in the direction you want the ball to roll (see Figure 7.6). Then align you putter to the label as you take your setup position.

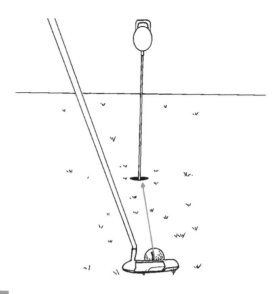

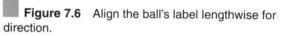

Figure 7.6 Align the ball's label lengthwise for direction.

PUTTING SUCCESS STOPPERS

Errors in putting are similar to those in the full swing and can be detected by watching the roll of the ball. The errors listed below are the most common ones in putting.

ERROR	CORRECTION
1. On straight putts, ball consistently rolls to side of hole.	1. a. Check your setup position: square clubface and body alignment. b. Use clubs on ground for direction; practice putting stroke using Track Drills (#3 and #4).
2. Putts land too far past the hole.	2. a. Maintain a firm, unitary swing of shoulders, arms, hands, and putter through the ball rather than using your wrists. b. Practice Cluster Putting Drill (# 9).
3. Putts come up short of hole.	3. Make backswing and forwardswing equal.
4. On downhill putts, ball consistently misses to left of the hole (for right-handed putter).	4. a. You aim putts offline. Check setup position for eyes directly over ball and alignment (use Eye Alignment Drill [# 2]). b. Practice green reading using the Green Clock Drill (#12).

PUTTING

DRILLS

1. Arm Swing Drill

The precision of the putting stroke is enhanced by the compactness of the unitary swing and your posture with your eyes over the ball.

a. Without a putter or ball, take your posture position. Bend your arms at the elbows and place your palms together. Swing your hands, arms, and shoulders, back and forth as a unit without moving your lower back. Use a 1-to-1 swing length.

b. Repeat (a) with a putter. When you add the putter, it becomes part of the unitary swing. The grip pressure is firm, but not tight, to prevent the hands from moving.

Success Goal = 10 total swings, feeling the unit

   a. 5 swings without putter _____

   b. 5 swings with putter _____

Success Check

• Maintain unit, hands, arms, and shoulders _____

• Pendular motion _____

To Increase Difficulty

• Practice with your eyes closed.

2. Eye Alignment Drill

The position of your eyes over the ball or target line increases your ability to visualize the path of the club and maintain a square stroke. You can check your eye position this way: With a club and ball, take your setup over the ball. Hold your putter in your dominant hand and an extra ball in your target hand. Move the putter from behind the ball on the ground and drop the extra ball from the bridge of your nose. The ball should fall on top of, or slightly behind, the other ball, but still on the target line.

Success Goal = 10 repetitions with correct form, dropped ball landing on other ball or target line 7 of 10 times _____

Success Check

• Maintain your posture position _____

To Increase Difficulty

• Modify Success Goal to landing on other ball or target line 9 of 10 times.

3. Consistent Path Track Drill

Developing a consistent path improves your directional control. Place two clubs on the ground parallel to the target line and just farther apart than your putter blade. Practice swinging the putter between the clubs, using a pendulum motion and maintaining a square blade as it moves back and forth.

Success Goal = 20 putting strokes without hitting either of parallel clubs ____

Success Check
- Maintain a square shoulder alignment ____
- Feel pendular motion, hands, arms, shoulder unit ____

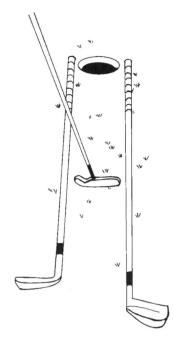

To Increase Difficulty
- Practice with eyes closed.
- Practice with rear and target arm separately than as a unit.

To Decrease Difficulty
- Modify success goal to require not hitting the clubs 14 of 20 times.

4. Track to Hole Drill

With the ends of the extra alignment clubs next to a hole, practice putting into the hole. Begin from about 1 foot away from the hole and gradually move back to 6 feet away.

Success Goal = 30 consecutive total putts made
- 10 consecutive putts from 1 foot ____
- 10 consecutive putts from 3 feet ____
- 10 consecutive putts from 6 feet ____

Success Check
- Maintain unit ____
- Hold follow-through, check position ____

To Increase Difficulty
- Putt with eyes closed.
- Extend distances in units 1 foot every 5 successful putts (Success Goal should be 60% for 4 to 6 feet).

To Decrease Difficulty
- Reduce Success Goal to 21 consecutive putts, 7 putts from each distance.

5. Varying the Distance Drill

Remove the tracks and practice putting balls, starting at 1 foot from the hole and moving back to 6 feet. Then alternate distances from 2, 5, 3, 1, 4, and 6 feet.

Success Goal = 30 total putts from 1-6 feet away from hole

4 putts from 1 foot ____
4 putts from 2 feet ____
4 putts from 3 feet ____
4 putts from 4 feet ____
4 putts from 5 feet ____
4 putts from 6 feet ____
6 putts alternating distances ____

Success Check

• Maintain unit ____

To Increase Difficulty

• Putt with eyes closed.
• Alter distance to 2,4,6, and 8 feet.
• Putt one putt from each distance, then repeat with Success Goal of 30 total putts, making 50% at each distance.

To Decrease Difficulty

• Modify success goal to 30 total points.

6. Tape Drill Without Ball

Learning to control the swing length of your stroke is important in developing consistent distance control. Place a 12-inch piece of tape on the floor, carpet, or green. Make a perpendicular mark across the tape in its center (at 6 inches). On either side of the mark, measure and mark 2, 4, and 6 inches away from the center. Label the marks 1, 2, 3 going away from the center in both directions.

Practice putting without a ball, making swing lengths of 1-to-1, 2-to-2, and 3-to-3 as marked on the tape.

Success Goal = 15 total strokes

5 strokes, 1-to-1 swing length ____
5 strokes, 3-to-3 swing length ____
5 strokes, 2-to-2 swing length ____

Success Check

• Hold finish to check for square blade unit intact ____

To Increase Difficulty

• Alternate repetitions with and without tape.
• Alternate swing lengths with each stroke.

To Decrease Difficulty

• Practice the 1-to-1 and 3-to-3 swing lengths.

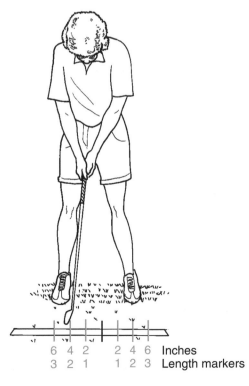

| 6 4 2 | 2 4 6 | Inches |
| 3 2 1 | 1 2 3 | Length markers |

7. Tape Drill With Ball

Place ball adjacent to 0 on the tape. Practice putting balls from the tape. Before each putt, take one practice stroke away from the ball the same swing length you will use to hit the ball. Then step up to the ball and actually stroke it, using the same swing length as the practice stroke.

Success Goal = 15 total putts, using practice stroke before each

5 putts, 1-to-1 swing length ____
5 putts, 3-to-3 swing length ____
5 putts, 2-to-2 swing length ____

Success Check

• Monitor finish, checking action of hands, arms, and shoulders ____

To Increase Difficulty

• Alternate repetitions with and without tape, noting distance consistency.
• Alternate repetitions with eyes closed.

To Decrease Difficulty

• Modify Success Goal to 9 total putts.

8. Putting Ladder Drill

Practice your stroke, checking for a square blade at finish and noting the distance the ball goes with each swing length.

Place five clubs in a ladder formation. The first club should be 10 feet away, with the other clubs at 3-foot intervals (10,13,16,19, and 22 feet). Practice putting for distance; don't worry about aiming at a specific target or hole. For example, decide to putt a ball between the second and third clubs (rungs) on the ladder.

Success Goal = putting 15 total balls, attempting to make the balls quit rolling between the desired club distances

2 putts between 10 and 13 feet ____
2 putts between 13 and 16 feet ____
2 putts between 16 and 19 feet ____
2 putts between 19 and 22 feet ____
2 putts between 22 and 25 feet ____
5 putts alternating distances, imagining you are on a course ____

Success Check

• Hold, finish, watch the ball until it stops ____
• Match the distance the ball rolled with how the stroke felt ____

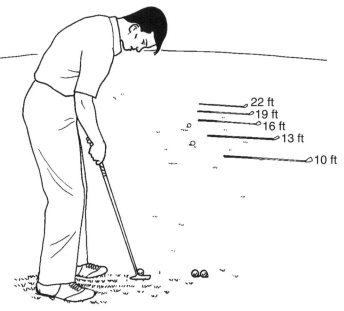

To Increase Difficulty

• Reduce target area to 1 foot.
• Putt with eyes closed.
• Add accuracy to Success Goal, requiring putt to roll between two desired club distances 9 out of 15 putts.

To Decrease Difficulty

• Increase distance between targets to 4 feet.

9. Cluster Putting Drill

Judging distance when putting depends on having a stroke that can be repeated. Your ability to feel the stroke can be improved through practice on this drill.

Take 3 balls. Without watching its roll, putt the first ball far enough so that it lands outside your peripheral vision. Still without looking, putt the next 2 balls, trying to have the balls come to rest in a cluster, nudging each other. For every group of 3 putts, try to cluster the second and third putts around the first. Focus on developing the feel of a repeating stroke.

Success Goal = 15 total putts, focusing on developing a feel for the repeated stroke and hitting the first ball in each group of 3 to a new distance

3 putts to location A (balls 1-3) _____
3 putts to location B (balls 4-6) _____
3 putts to location C (balls 7-9) _____
3 putts to location D (balls 10-12) _____
3 putts to location E (balls 13-16) _____

Success Check

• Focus on the swing length and pace _____

To Increase Difficulty

• Putt with eyes closed.
• Add accuracy element, balls cluster within a 3-foot circle of first ball, at new distance.

To Decrease Difficulty

• Look at the distance each ball rolls.
• Use 4 balls instead of 3 and alternate looking at the distance the ball rolls and keeping your eyes closed.

10. Line Drill

To practice short putts and controlling the length of your putting backswing, place 6 balls 1 foot apart on the target line to the hole. Starting with the ball closest to the hole, putt the balls into the hole. When a putt is missed, start again with all 6 balls. Align the label of each ball before starting to putt.

Success Goal = 5 repetitions of making 6 consecutive putts

6 made out of 6 putts _____   6 made out of 6 putts _____
6 made out of 6 putts _____   6 made out of 6 putts _____
6 made out of 6 putts _____

Success Check

• Maintain unit ____
• Check finish for blade alignment and result ____

To Increase Difficulty

• Putt with eyes closed.
• Putt from uneven slopes.

To Decrease Difficulty

• Modify Success Goal to 3 repetitions.
• Reduce number of balls made to 5 of 6.

11. Target Hand Low Drill

The purpose of the target hand low drill is to reduce wrist motion in your stroke. If on the finish of your stroke, the clubhead is in front of your hands or your rear hand has changed position relative to its initial position in the setup, your wrists have been too active.

Hold the putter with the target hand at the bottom end of the grip, and hold it against the target forearm with the rear hand. Make practice strokes feeling the shaft and target arm as one. The club shaft should maintain full contact with the target forearm throughout the stroke. If the club shaft comes off the forearm at any point during the stroke, you are using your wrists too much. Position the ball under your target shoulder.

Success Goal = 12 total putts, using the Line Drill (#10) with 2 practice swings between each putt

   2 target hand low ____
   2 regular grip ____
   1 target hand low ____
   1 regular grip ____

✔ *Success Check*

• Maintain the shaft against the target forearm ____
• Feel the pendular motion ____

To Increase Difficulty

• Practice the Cluster Putting Drill (#9).
• Practice the Ladder Drill (#8).

To Decrease Difficulty

• Modify Success Goal to 6 total putts, 3 target hand low and 3 regular grip.

12. Green Clock Drill

Through systematic practice of watching balls roll on a green with various degrees of slope, you begin to be able to predict putt curvature. Once you start predicting ball roll, compare what you thought would happen with what actually occurs.

Find a green that slopes significantly. Place 12 balls 5 feet away from the hole in a circle, spacing balls like numerals on a clock face. Start putting at the lowest point on the slope (6 o'clock). Read the green and go through your entire setup procedure with each putt. Continue to putt in a counterclockwise direction (i.e., 5, 4, 3, and so on). Take careful note of the roll of each ball.

Success Goal = 15 total putts, charting the curvature of each putt by drawing dotted lines on the clock face and from different positions, imagining you're on the course as you putt each one

Putts going in hole _____
Putts coming up short of hole _____
Putts going beyond hole (too long) _____
Putts missing hole to right _____
Putts missing hole to left _____
Putts made imagining on course _____

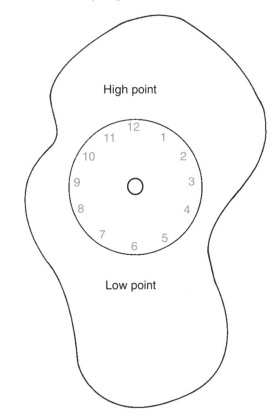

Success Check

• Visualize the roll of the ball before each stroke _____
• Preset your alignment with the ball label _____
• Trust your feel of distances _____

To Increase Difficulty

• Alternate distance around the hole.
• Imagine you're putting with a friend for a coke.
• Practice putting and compete with a friend.
• Imagine you're on the course as you practice putting from different distances.

To Decrease Difficulty

• Reduce the number of putts from 12 to 8.
• Chart alternate putts.

PUTTING SUCCESS SUMMARY

After doing the drills, are you a better putter than you thought? Most players are good in one or two of the areas. Having a method to identify your weaknesses and ways to improve will help you develop greater consistency. Go easy on yourself—not even the pros make all those 3-foot putts. Remember the basic stroke is your number one priority. Distance control (force) is the second most important, and reading greens is third. With skill in all three, your number of strokes on the green will decrease markedly.

Through the drills in this step, you can identify your strengths and weaknesses. Continue to refine your strengths while focusing on your weaknesses. Ask your practice partner, golf pro, teacher, or another trained observer to qualitatively evaluate your technique according to the checklist in Figure 7.3.

STEP 8

SAND SHOTS: GETTING UNTRAPPED

The "easiest shot" in golf is presented in this step. The sand shot from bunkers around the green is often preferred by very good players over hitting a pitch shot of 30 yards or hitting from the rough around the green. In hitting this shot, you don't have to contact the ball. You hit the sand and the ball flies out of the bunker with the sand.

There are three conditions in the sand that you will not face when the ball is on the fairway or rough: (a) the lie—the ball either rests on top of the sand or is partially buried below the sand's surface; (b) stance stability; and (c) the club does not contact the ball directly but the sand, which pushes the ball out of the bunker.

In this step you learn how to utilize your full swing motion effectively in the sand by modifying your setup. This lets you accommodate the three sand conditions in executing the two sand shots: the *explosion shot* and the *buried lie shot*.

Why Are Sand Shots Important?

Sand bunkers (formerly called "sandtraps") are strategically placed on courses in the landing areas where the majority of players hit their tee shots and around the greens. The frequency of your use of sand shots depends on the course or courses you play. The number of sand bunkers on a given course can range from none to 100 or more.

Your ability to consistently hit out of bunkers helps you develop confidence and save strokes during a round of golf. For many players, the sight of sand causes a panic button to go off. This doesn't need to happen to you.

When your ball lands in a sand bunker, the generally soft texture of the sand creates a hitting surface and ball lie that are different from those found on the fairway or with the grass conditions on which you have thus far practiced. The sand also adds the challenges of your maintaining your balance during the swing and adapting to the rules that prohibit you from letting your club touch the sand before your forwardswing.

Your understanding of the modifications needed in the setup position and the use of the sand wedge to allow for the different sand textures can help you become an overall better golfer.

How to Execute the Sand Shots

The sandwedge is the club specifically designed for use in the sand but is also used for other shots. This club differs from other irons in that it is slightly heavier and the sole, or bottom, of the club is wider and angles down with the back edge lower than the front edge of the club (see Figure 8.1). The differences in club design make it easier to swing through the sand. The texture of the sand, though soft, is heavier than grass and offers greater resistance when contacted during the swing.

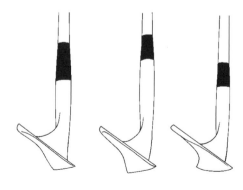

Figure 8.1 Types of sand wedges. Notice the differences in the soles.

There are two basic sand shots: The *explosion shot* and the *buried lie shot*; the lie of the ball in the sand determines which one is selected (see Figure 8.2). When the ball rests on top of the sand, more similar to a ball in the fairway, the explosion shot is used. The buried lie shot is used, as the name implies, when the ball is partially buried or rests completely below the level of the sand. Each shot will be discussed separately, with special note of the specific modifications in the setup positions from that of the full swing.

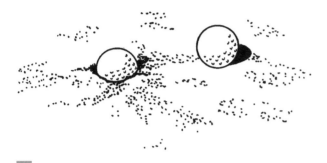

Figure 8.2 Ball buried (left) and ball on top of sand (right).

You should know the following rule and etiquette when your ball goes in the sand (refer to a current *USGA Rule Book* for more detail):

Rule 13.4: The club is not allowed to touch the sand prior to the forwardswing motion. Touching the sand prior to contacting the ball results in a two-stroke penalty.

You can remove anything man made. If the ball moves when you remove the obstacle, it must be replaced (i.e., cans, bottles, rake, etc.).

Etiquette: Carry the rake into the sand and place it out of the way, points up, to avoid testing the texture of the sand. Rake the sand before leaving and place the rake, points down for safety, either in the bunker along the side or just outside the bunker.

Explosion Shot

The explosion shot is similar to an iron shot from the fairway. There are three setup modifications from the pitch shot affecting clubface alignment, body alignment, and stance. The clubface is slightly open and aligned to the target for the explosion. The open clubface avoids digging into the sand too deeply. Before gripping the club, open the clubface slightly; then take your neutral grip position.

Your body alignment should be slightly open to the target line, rather than square as in the full swing. This adjustment counteracts the influence of the open clubface (Step 4), producing a straight shot rather than a push.

The stance modification provides you greater stability during the swing (see Figure 8.3a). As you take your stance, dig your toes into the sand a few inches. This places more weight toward the balls of your feet. By placing your feet below the level of the sand, as you make your pitch swing, the club enters the sand several inches to the rear side of the ball position. To avoid touching the sand, hold the club slightly above the sand as you take your setup.

These setup modifications allow you to use your pitch swing motion in the sand (see Figures 8.3, b and c). The trajectory of the explosion shot is fairly high, and the ball lands with little roll. The sandwedge (SW) by design is the most effective club for the explosion shot. However, a pitching wedge (PW) or 9-iron can also be used. Directional and distance control come with practice and experience.

FIGURE 8.3 **KEYS TO SUCCESS**

EXPLOSION SAND SHOT

(*indicates difference from basic pitch shot motion)

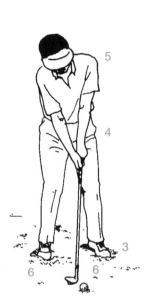

a

b

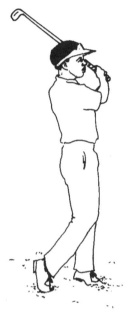

c

Preparation

1. Neutral Grip (Vs in grip pointing rear of chin) ___
2. Feet shoulder width apart; weight evenly distributed ___
*3. Feet aligned open to target line ___
*4. Hips aligned open to target line ___
*5. Shoulders aligned open to target line ___
*6. Toes dug into sand ___
7. Ball position center to target side ___
8. Blade of club aligns to target ___

Execution

1. Arms, hands, and club start as unit ___
2. Weight shifts to rear on backswing ___
3. Wrists cocked at hip level ___
4. Hips turn to rear followed by back to target ___
5. Hands even with rear shoulder ___
*6. Backswing length 3 or 4 ___
7. Weight shifts to target side on forwardswing ___
8. Arms, hands, club start down as a unit ___
9. Wrists uncock at hip level ___
10. Arms, hands, and club extended at impact ___
11. Wrists recock by target-side hip level___
12. Hips turned to target ___

Follow-Through

1. Weight on target side (rear knee toward target knee) ___
2. Hips face target ___
3. Chest to target ___
4. Forwardswing length 3 or 4 ___
5. Balanced finish ___

Buried Lie Sand Shot

The buried lie shot differs in the setup position and in the follow-through from the explosion shot and the pitch swing because the club must swing down more steeply, digging into the sand to pop the ball out from the buried lie. The setup position is similar to the chip shot, but using a backswing length of 3 as in the pitch shot. There are five setup modifications from the pitch swing—in stance, body alignment, weight distribution, clubface alignment, and ball position.

Your stance for the buried lie shot is the same as in the explosion shot, with your toes dug several inches into the sand for stability. With this position, as indicated with the explosion shot, the club enters the sand to the rear side of center. Your body alignment is slightly open for your feet and hips, while your shoulders are square to the target line. Your

weight distribution is to the target side, with the upper and lower body leaning toward the target. This is the same position as in the chip shot. The clubface position is square, but delofted because the ball position is to the rear side of center, just forward of the point where the club enters the sand (see Figure 8.4a).

The forwardswing motion is like your longer chip shot but with wrist motion (see Figure 8.4b). The sand will restrict your follow-through, creating a similar position as your chip shot with the target wrist straight and the rear wrist bent (see Figure 8.4c).

The modifications in this setup position and the restricted follow-through for the buried lie shot produce a shot with a low trajectory and a lot of roll. A sand wedge, pitching wedge, or 9-iron are effective. A higher trajectory is possible with the sand wedge, which should be used whenever possible for the buried lie shot. However, it will tend to be lower than the explosion shot.

FIGURE 8.4 **KEYS TO SUCCESS**

BURIED LIE SAND SHOT
(*indicates difference from pitch shot motion)

Front View

a   b   c

Side View
(Buried lie)

a

b

c

Preparation

1. Grip club in neutral position ___
2. Feet shoulder width apart ___
3. Open foot and hip alignment ___
4. Square shoulder alignment ___
*5. Weight on target side (hands and head) ___
*6. Toes dug into sand ___
*7. Ball position center to rear side___
*8. Square blade (delofted) ___

Execution

1. Arms, hands, club swing back as unit ___
2. Weight shifts to rear on backswing ___
3. Wrists cocked at hip level ___
4. Hips turn to rear; back to target ___
*5. Backswing length 3 or 4 ___
6. Weight shifts to target side on forwardswing___
7. Arms, hands, club start down as unit ___
8. Wrists uncocked at hip level ___
9. Arms extended at ball contact with wrists bent___
10. Wrists restricted at target-side hip level ___

Follow-Through

1. Weight on target side ___
*2. Hold partial side orientation ___
*3. Forwardswing length 2 or 3 ___
4. Hold position at end to check for balance ___

SAND SHOT SUCCESS STOPPERS

Sand shots can be analyzed by looking at two different situations: Explosion Shots and Buried Lie Shots. To detect problems with these shots, it is important to differentiate between them. The explosion shot is similar to an iron shot from the fairway, while the buried lie shot is different from the full swing motion because the club must swing down more steeply in order to dig into the sand to pop up the ball. The errors listed below are the most common problems from the sand.

ERROR	CORRECTION
Explosion Shot	
1. Your swing takes too much sand, and the ball does not come out of the trap consistently.	1. a. Check ball position. b. Practice Line Drill (#1), noting consistent contact point. c. Position ball in stance 1 to 2 inches to target side of point where you contact sand. d. Maintain arm position.
2. You hit the ball instead of the sand behind the ball.	2. a. Check setup and ball position. b. Practice Line Drill (#1); focus on a line 1 to 2 inches behind ball in contacting sand.
Buried Lie Sand Shot	
1. Shots fly out of sand and go too far, even though sand seems to be properly displaced.	1. Practice the Bunker Distance Control Drill (#7), working on swing pace.
2. Ball scoots off in direction of a push, having been hit by hosel.	2. Check setup position, alignment, and ball position. Alignment may be too open and ball position too far back in your stance.

DRILLS

1. Line Practice Explosion Sand Shot Drill

The key to sand shots is to contact the sand in the same point in your swing each time. This helps you develop confidence in swinging through the sand, making the ball fly out with the sand. Practice this Line Drill to aid in developing this feel and consistency.

a. Draw a line in the sand and take your setup position for the explosion shot. Place the line in the center of your stance. Make practice swings without balls, moving up the line after each swing. Note where you contact the sand in relation to the line. Be sure to practice your entire setup procedure prior to each swing.

b. Draw a new line where you where consistently hitting the sand in part (a). Place 5 balls 2 inches in front (target side) of the new line. Be sure each ball is resting on top of the sand. Practice hitting through the line and watching the balls fly out of the sand. Do not worry about the direction or distance of your shots. Remember, your first objective is to get out of the sand. The order of club preference is SW, PW, and 9-iron.

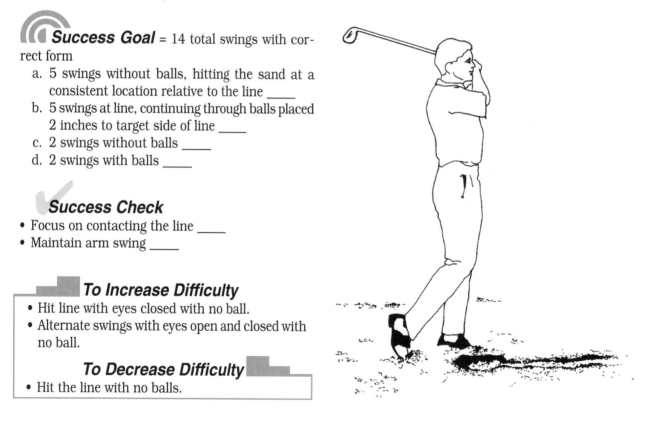

Success Goal = 14 total swings with correct form
   a. 5 swings without balls, hitting the sand at a consistent location relative to the line ____
   b. 5 swings at line, continuing through balls placed 2 inches to target side of line ____
   c. 2 swings without balls ____
   d. 2 swings with balls ____

Success Check
• Focus on contacting the line ____
• Maintain arm swing ____

To Increase Difficulty
• Hit line with eyes closed with no ball.
• Alternate swings with eyes open and closed with no ball.

To Decrease Difficulty
• Hit the line with no balls.

2. Line Practice Buried Lie Sand Shot Drill

The key to sand shots is to contact the sand within a few inches of the same point in your swing each time. This helps you develop confidence in swinging through the sand, making the ball fly out with the sand. Practice the Line Drill this time with a buried lie to aid in developing this feel and consistency.

a. Draw a line in the sand and take your setup position for the buried lie sand shot. Place the line in the center of your stance. Make practice swings without balls, moving up the line after each swing. Note where you contact the sand in relation to the line. Be sure to practice your entire setup procedure prior to each swing.

b. Draw a new line where you were consistently hitting the sand in part (a). Place 5 buried balls 2 inches in front (target side) of the new line. Be sure each ball is resting on top of the sand. Practice hitting through the line and watching the balls fly out of the sand. Do not worry about the direction or distance of your shots. Remember, your first objective is to get out of the sand. The order of club preference is SW, PW, and 9-iron.

Success Goal = 14 total swings with correct form
    a. 5 swings without balls, hitting the sand at a consistent location relative to the line ____
    b. 5 swings at line, continuing through balls placed 2 inches to target side of line ____
    c. 2 swings without balls ____
    d. 2 swings with balls ____

Success Check
• Focus on contacting the line ____
• Maintain arm swing ____

To Increase Difficulty
• Hit lines with eyes closed with no ball.
• Alternate swings with eyes open and closed with no ball.

To Decrease Difficulty
• Hit the line with no balls.

3. Fried Egg Visual Image for Explosion Sand Shot Drill

Some golfers like to imagine that a golf ball sitting in the sand is like a fried egg. You want to imagine putting the spatula under the yolk of the egg without breaking the yolk.

Draw an oval in the sand. Imagine that a golf ball in its center is the yolk of an egg. Take your stance with the entire "egg" in the center of your stance. Hit the ball out, thinking about the club as a spatula scraping the egg off the bottom of the frying pan, scraping under the yolk so as not to break it. Draw 5 of these ovals in the sand and place a ball in the center of each.

Success Goal = hitting each "egg" out of the sand
    a. 2 swings hitting edge of egg white ____
    b. 3 swings hitting fried egg with ball ____

Success Check
• Hit sand at edge of the white of the egg and go through the yolk ____
• Continue swing ____

4. Rules Situation Drill

There are many situations on the golf course where it is important to know the rules and what options you may have. For example, on the first hole your ball lands in the sand. It is resting next to a pine cone with a good lie. What are your options?

Success Goal = respond to the following True-False questions using the rule book as needed:

*a. The pine cone may be removed ____
*b. You may take practice swings hitting the sand ____
*c. There is a one-stroke penalty for hitting the sand on the forwardswing ____

*Answers: a: false; b: false; c: false

Success Check

• Refer to Rule 13-4 ____

To Increase Difficulty

• Respond to the True-False questions without using the rule book, then check your answers.
• Rewrite any false statement, making it true.

5. Overlapping Grip Explosion Shot Drill

One common tendency in hitting sand shots is for the arms to decelerate because the target arm slows down. To feel the target arm throughout the swing, practice this drill.

a. Take your setup position for the explosion shot. Grip the club with your target hand, then place your rear hand on top of your target hand. Practice swinging the club 10 times, and knocking sand out of the bunker using the line drill directions for the explosion shot (Drill 1).

b. Draw a new line at the point where you consistently hit the sand in part (a). Place 5 balls 2 inches toward the target side of the new line. Hit the sand and balls out of the bunker.

Success Goal = 15 swings with correct form
5 swings hitting sand in same spot 3 of 5 times ____
5 swings hitting line and continuing through balls ____
5 swings regular grip and no line ____

Success Check

• Focus on contacting the sand first ____
• Feel both arms swing through or past the line ____

To Increase Difficulty

• Practice with eyes closed and no ball.
• Alternate between overlap and regular grip, hitting balls only.

To Decrease Difficulty

• Reduce swings with overlap to 3.

6. Overlapping Grip: Buried Lie Shot Drill

Take your setup position for the buried lie shot. Place a line in the center of your stance. Grip the club with your target hand, then place your rear hand on top of your target hand as in the previous drill.

a. Take 5 swings without balls in the setup position for the buried lie shot. Note where the club strikes the sand on each swing.

b. Draw a new line in the sand at the point where you consistently hit the sand in part (a). Now slightly bury 5 balls on the line drawn in the sand. Be sure each ball is slightly buried. Practice hitting the line and the ball out of the sand while using the overlapping grip. Focus your attention on feeling your target arm continue to swing throughout the swing.

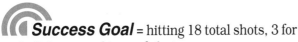 **Success Goal** = 15 total swings with proper setup

    5 swings hitting sand at consistent location relative to line ____

    5 swings at balls slightly buried on target line ____

    5 swings, regular grip, no line ____

To Increase Difficulty
- Make practice swings with target arm only.
- Alternate between explosion shot and buried lie shot.

To Decrease Difficulty
- Reduce number of balls.

Success Check
- Maintain upper body lean ____
- Focus on the club entering the sand ____

7. Bunker Distance Control Drill

Distance control in the sand can be practiced in the same ways as pitching, chipping, and putting. Establish four targets 10, 15, and 20 yards away. Practice adjusting your swing length or speed to produce a sand shot that carries to each of those target distances.

a. Using an explosion shot, hit 3 balls to each target.

b. Using a buried lie shot, hit 3 balls to each target.

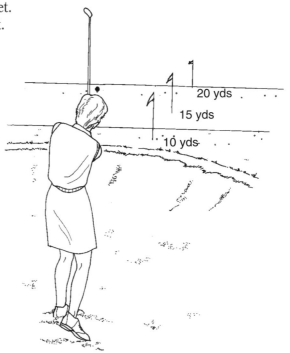

Success Goal = hitting 18 total shots, 3 for each distance and type of shot

  a. Explosion Shot

    3 balls hit at 10-yard target ____

    3 balls hit at 15-yard target ____

    3 balls hit at 20-yard target ____

  b. Buried Lie Sand Shot

    3 balls hit at 10-yard target ____

    3 balls hit at 15-yard target ____

    3 balls hit at 20-yard target ____

Success Check
- Trust yourself—ball rides out with the sand ____

To Increase Difficulty

- Alternate distances with each shot.
- Alternate explosion shot and buried lies:
  a. use same distances.
  b. use different distances.

To Decrease Difficulty

- Hit explosion shots 10 and 15 yards only.
- Hit buried lie shots 10 and 20 yards only.

SAND SHOTS SUCCESS SUMMARY

Executing sand shots is not difficult if you (a) access the lie of the ball as resting either on sand or below the sand; (b) select the appropriate shot for the lie (the explosion shot for those on top of the sand and the buried lie shot for those below the surface of the sand); and (c) modify your setup position according to the type of shot needed. Use the following summary comparison chart to review the differences between the full swing and both the buried lie and the explosion sand shots. Then ask a friend or practice partner to assess your ability to execute each of these shots by using the Keys to Success in Figures 8.3 and 8.4. Remember the key idea with both sand shots is to swing through the sand. Asterisks denote the differences in the sand shot from the full swing motion.

Summary Comparison Chart	
Explosion Shot	**Buried Lie Shot**
Setup	
• Ball on top of sand • Feet aligned open to target • Hips aligned open to target • Shoulders aligned open to target • Toes dug into sand	• Ball below surface of sand • Weight on target side (upper body lean toward target) • Square blade (delofted) • Ball position, center to rear • Toes dug into sand • Shoulders square to target
Backswing	
• Swing length 3 or 4	• Swing length 3 or 4
Forwardswing	
• Regular forwardswing	• Arms extended at ball contact, with rear wrist bent • Arms and wrists restricted when reach target side hip level
Follow-Through	
• Hips and chest face target • Swing length 3 or 4	• Hold partial-side orientation • Swing length 2 or 3

STEP 9

UNEVEN LIES: ADJUSTING FOR TERRAIN

One of the distinguishing features of a golf course is the type of terrain on which it is built. This varies from one geographical area to another as well as within the design of the course itself. For example, the courses in Florida or Holland tend to be flat, while those in Vermont or Austria are usually hilly. Playing on different types of terrain creates a challenge to golfers.

In the previous steps, you have been practicing on relatively flat terrain, similar to Florida's, in which the ball and your feet have been on the same level. When you practice or play courses in mountainous areas or where there are hills or slopes, there are times when the ball and your feet are on different levels. These situations are called *uneven lies* and require modifications in your setup position.

Two types of uneven lies are presented in this step: *sidehill lies* and *uphill* or *downhill lies*.

When the ball comes to rest in a nice, flat, grassy area, it is referred to as a *good lie*. In contrast, balls that land on uphill or downhill lies and sidehill lies are sometimes referred to as trouble shots. In fact, though, they are "trouble" only if you do not practice them and understand the effects of these lies on your setup and on the action of the ball.

Why Are Uneven Lies Important?

Not all golf courses are flat. Knowledge of how to adjust the setup position for the various lies helps to reduce the anxiety of playing on hills. Unfortunately, not all practice areas have hills or slopes on which to practice these types of shots. However, with just a basic understanding of how to play the shots, you will find that you can quickly adapt to uneven terrain.

How to Execute Uneven Lies

The location of the ball relative to your feet distinguishes the two types of lies, sidehill and uphill/downhill lies. In sidehill lies, the ball is either above or below your feet (see Figures 9.1a and b); in the uphill and downhill lies, the ball is even with your feet (see Figures 9.2a and b).

The full swing motion you learned in Step 3, using swing lengths of 5-to-5 or 4-to-4, is appropriate for most uneven lies. The swing length is determined by the degree of slope and the distance to the desired

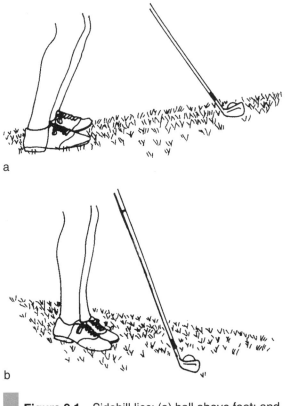

a

b

Figure 9.1 Sidehill lies: (a) ball above feet; and (b) ball below feet.

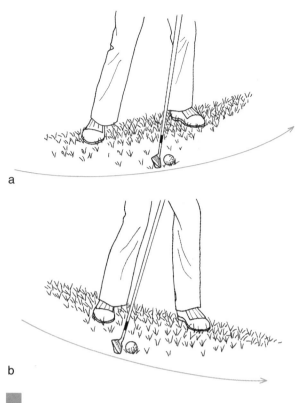

a

b

Figure 9.2 (a) Uphill lie; and (b) downhill lie.

target area. The more severe the slope, the greater the demand for balance and control, which limits your swing length and potential distance achieved.

The major difference in the uneven and the regular fairway shots is in the setup position modifica-tions due to the terrain. The sidehill lies and the uphill/downhill lies are now discussed separately, with specific note given to their differences in setup.

Sidehill Lies

Sidehill lies have the ball either above or below your feet when you take your stance. These lies differ slightly in the setup position from your regular full swing with an iron. Both sidehill lies require adjust-ment to an intermediate target rather than directly on the primary target, because the natural ball flight from sidehill lies tends to curve in the downward di-rection of the slope. If the ball is above your feet, it tends to hook; if below your feet, it tends to slice. As you take your setup position, select an intermediate target about 10 yards to the right or left of the de-sired target, depending on the lie.

If the ball position is above (higher than) your feet, it requires one additional setup modification. Because the hill is closer to your hands as you set up, grip the club about 3 inches from the top; then execute your regular swing. This "choked-up" grip should be adjusted based on the degree of slope.

When the ball is positioned below your feet, as you swing, gravity tends to impair your balance more than the other lies. To enhance your balance, place more weight toward your heels, rather than on the midstep to the balls of your feet as in your regular swing (see Figure 9.3).

FIGURE
9.3 **KEYS TO SUCCESS**

SIDEHILL LIES
(*indicates differences from basic full swing motion)

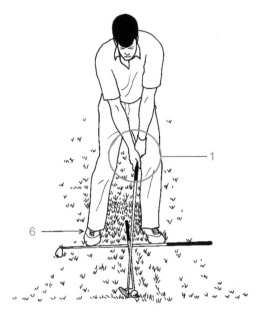

Ball Above Feet

Preparation

*1. Neutral Grip: Choked-up grip ___
2. Feet shoulder width apart ___
3. Square foot alignment ___
4. Square hip alignment ___
5. Square shoulder alignment ___
6. Weight distribution: even
7. Posture over ball, with flat back ___
8. Eyes over hands ___
9. Ball position
   • irons: center of stance ___
   • woods: target side of center ___
10. Square blade ___

Ball Below Feet

Preparation

*1. Neutral Grip: Full length on club ___
2. Feet shoulder width apart ___
3. Square foot alignment ___
4. Square hip alignment ___
5. Square shoulder alignment ___
*6. Weight distribution: toward heels ___
7. Posture over ball, with flat back ___
8. Eyes over hands ___
9. Ball position
   • irons: forward of stance ___
   • woods: target side of center ___
10. Square blade ___

(Ball above feet)

Execution

1. Arms, hands, club start as unit ___
2. Weight shifts to rear on backswing (target knee toward rear knee) ___
3. Wrists cocked at hip level ___
4. Hips turn to rear on backswing ___
5. Back to target on backswing ___
6. Backswing length 4 or 5 ___
7. Weight shifts to target side ___
8. Arms, hands, club start down as unit ___
9. Wrists uncock at hip level ___
10. Arms, hands, club extended at contact ___
11. Wrists recocked at hip level ___
12. Hips turned to target ___

Follow-Through

1. Weight on target side ___
2. Hips face target ___
3. Chest to target ___
4. Forwardswing length 4 or 5 ___
5. Balanced ending ___

(Ball below feet)

Execution

1. Arms, hands, club start as unit ___
2. Weight shifts to rear on backswing (target knee toward rear knee) ___
3. Wrists cocked at hip level ___
4. Hips turn to rear on backswing ___
5. Back to target on backswing ___
6. Backswing length 4 or 5 ___
7. Weight shifts to target side ___
8. Arms, hands, club start down as unit ___
9. Wrists uncock at hip level ___
10. Arms, hands, club extended at contact ___
11. Wrists recocked at hip level ___
12. Hips turned to target ___

Follow-Through

1. Weight on target side ___
2. Hips face target ___
3. Chest to target ___
4. Forwardswing length 4 or 5 ___
5. Balanced ending ___

Uphill and Downhill Lies

In uphill and downhill lies, the ball is even with your feet in your stance—the only thing is, your feet are at different levels on a slope. In an uphill lie, your forwardswing must go up the slope (i.e., to the top of the slope); in a downhill lie, your forwardswing must go down the slope (i.e., to the bottom of the slope).

These lies require four modifications of your full swing setup positions. The alignment requires an intermediate target, as with the sidehill lie (previously discussed), because the slope affects the ball flight. Uphill lie shots tend to draw; downhill lie shots tend to fade. Grip the club in a choked-up position about 3 inches from the top. This choked-up position is necessary because your hands are closer to the slope on both lies. The ball position is closer to the level of the high foot on the slope. Move away from the ball and take several practice swings. Be sure to maintain the same slope angle as you make your practice swings. Note where the club contacts the ground. This is your ball position. The practice swings also help you determine the amount of choking-up required. Position your shoulders parallel to the slope. This makes it easier to swing the club with the slope (see Figure 9.4).

FIGURE
9.4

KEYS TO SUCCESS

UPHILL AND DOWNHILL LIES

(*indicates difference from the basic full swing setup)

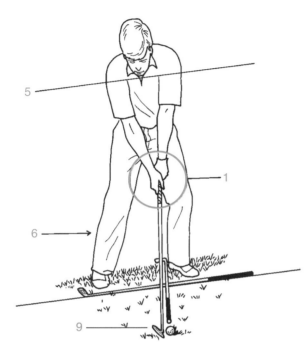
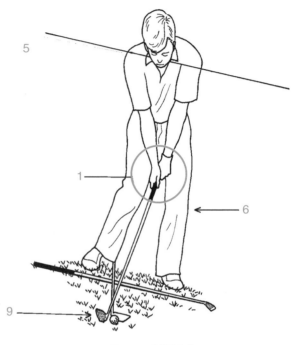

Uphill Lie	**Downhill Lie**
Preparation	**Preparation**

Uphill Lie	Downhill Lie
*1. Neutral grip, choked up about 3 inches ___	*1. Neutral grip, choked up about 3 inches ___
2. Feet shoulder width apart ___	2. Feet shoulder width apart ___
*3. Align to intermediate target ___	*3. Align to intermediate target ___
4. Square foot alignment ___	4. Square foot alignment ___
*5. Square shoulder alignment parallel to slope ___	*5. Square shoulder alignment parallel to slope ___
*6. Weight even over both feet (lean into hill) ___	*6. Weight even over both feet (lean into hill) ___
7. Posture over ball ___	7. Posture over ball ___
8. Weight forward, midstep to balls of feet ___	8. Weight forward, midstep to balls of feet ___
*9. Ball position toward high foot ___	*9. Ball position toward high foot ___
*10. Blade square to intermediate target line ___	*10. Blade square to intermediate target line ___

Execution 　　　　　　　　　　　　**Execution**

Execution	Execution
1. Arms, hands, club start as unit ___	1. Arms, hands, club start as unit ___
2. Weight shifts to rear on backswing ___	2. Weight shifts to rear on backswing ___
3. Wrists cocked at hip level ___	3. Wrists cocked at hip level ___
4. Hips turn to rear on backswing ___	4. Hips turn to rear on backswing ___
5. Back to target on backswing ___	5. Back to target on backswing ___
6. Backswing length 4 or 5 ___	6. Backswing length 4 or 5 ___

(Uphill lie)

7. Weight shifts to target side on forward-swing ___
8. Arms, hands, club start down as unit ___
9. Wrists uncocked at hip level ___
10. Arms, hands, club extended at contact ___
11. Wrists recocked at hip level ___
12. Hips turned to target ___

Follow-Through

1. Weight on target side ___
2. Hips face target ___
3. Chest to target ___
4. Swing length 4 or 5 ___
5. Balanced ending ___

(Downhill lie)

7. Weight shifts to target side on forward-swing ___
8. Arms, hands, club start down as unit ___
9. Wrists uncocked at hip level ___
10. Arms, hands, club extended at contact ___
11. Wrists recocked at hip level ___
12. Hips turned to target ___

Follow-Through

1. Weight on target side ___
2. Hips face target ___
3. Chest to target ___
4. Swing length 4 or 5 ___
5. Balanced ending ___

UNEVEN LIES SUCCESS STOPPERS

It is easier to hit uneven lie shots when you understand how they differ from flat shots. The most common problem of hitting from slopes is the tendency to set up as if it was a flat shot. The swing motion is the same as for the full swing, it is just that the setup is different. The Success Stoppers that follow will provide tips for avoiding typical errors.

ERROR	CORRECTION
Sidehill Lies	
1. You hit sidehill shots "fat" (stubbing club into ground) when the ball is above your feet.	1. a. Choke up (lower your grip) on club. b. Check ball position.
2. You top sidehill shots with ball below feet.	2. a. Check setup position; you may be sitting back too much on heels and losing your balance. b. Put weight on heels but maintain posture over ball (see Figure 9.3).
3. You consistently pull sidehill lies when ball is above feet.	3. a. Check alignment. b. Ball tends to curve in direction down slope (hook).
Uphill/Downhill Lies	
1. You top ball on downhill lies.	1. Maintain good posture throughout swing.
2. You hit downhill shots "fat" (stubbing club into ground).	2. a. Position shoulders parallel to slope. b. Position ball toward high foot.
3. You consistently pull uphill shots with wood.	3. a. Check setup alignment. b. Uphill lies tend to hook; be sure to use intermediate target (see Figure 9.4).

UNEVEN LIE

DRILLS

1. Setup Sidehill Lie Drill

To become familiar with the setup position for sidehill lies, find a sidehill from which to practice. Place two clubs on the grass, one lying straight up the slope, the other at right angles to this (review Figure 9.3). These clubs provide a reference for ball position and stance. Choose a target to the right or left of the horizontal club.

Using a 5-iron, modify your setup for the slope of the hill. Practice swings, noting the way your swing feels and the sensations of the swing. Do you feel balanced? Remember to choke up (grip club lower) whenever the ball is above your feet (see Figure a below). Or, if you find you pull sidehill lies when the ball is above your feet, then adjust your alignment to the target (see Figure b).

Success Goal = 10 total swings while noting balance on the follow-through

   3 swings from sidehill lies, balls below feet ___
     swings in balance ___
   2 swings from a flat lie ___
     swings in balance ___
   3 swings from sidehill lies, balls above feet ___
     swings in balance ___
   2 swings from a flat lie ___
     swings in balance ___

To Increase Difficulty
• Practice swings with your eyes shut.
• Alternate 3 swings between your normal setup and the sidehill lie to feel the difference.

To Decrease Difficulty
• Practice either above or below the feet only.
• Select either a 7- or 9- iron.

Success Check
• Focus on balance ___

a

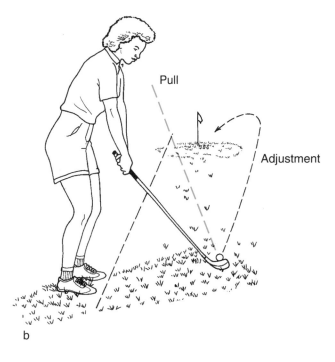

Pull

Adjustment

b

2. Uphill/Downhill Lie Drill

To become familiar with uphill and downhill lies, you may have to do some searching to find these lies. Place two clubs on the grass, one lying straight up the slope, the other at right angles to this (review Figure 9.4). The clubs provide a reference for ball position and stance. Choose targets to the high side of the club lying up the slope for the uphill lie and to the low side of this club for the downhill lie (see figure below).

Using a 5-iron, modify your setup for the slope of the hill. Note your sensations on the swing. You should feel as though swinging up the hill or down the hill. The severity of the slope may not allow complete balance as on a flat lie. Remember to maintain good posture throughout swing to avoid topping the ball on downhill lies.

Success Goal = 14 total swings, noting swing sensations with changes in the slope and contrast to a flat lie
  3 swings, downhill lie ___
  2 swings, flat lie ___
  3 swings, uphill lie ___
  2 swings, flat lie ___
  1 swing, downhill lie ___
  1 swing, flat lie ___
  1 swing, uphill lie ___
  1 swing, flat lie ___

Success Check

- Adjust to the slope _____
- Feel the contrast in a slope and a flat lie _____
- Make practice swings to feel balance _____

To Increase Difficulty

- Alternate swings with a wood.
- Hit balls to targets as the situation allows.

To Decrease Difficulty

- Select a less lofted club of your choice.
- Select one lie situation of your choice.

3. Single Bucket Drill

To gain an awareness of the desired ascending and descending angles of approach, on flat ground put one foot on a bucket or the edge of your golf bag. Note how each swing feels as the bucket or golf bag limits your lower body action and exaggerates the sense of ascent or descent of the swing.

a. To feel the descending angle of approach with the irons, take your regular setup position for the full swing with a ball in the center of your stance and on a tee. Place your rear foot on the bucket (see Figure a, next page). Hit balls using a 7-iron, noting how it feels.

b. To feel the ascending angle, take your regular setup position with the ball on a tee toward your target side. Place your target-side foot on the bucket (see Figure b, next page). Hit balls with a 5-iron or 7-wood.

Success Goal = 10 total swings, alternating with a flat lie

   3 swings with a 7-iron, your rear foot on bucket ___

   2 swings, flat lie ___

   3 swings with a 5- or 7-wood, ball on tee, target-side foot on bucket ___

   2 swings, flat lie ___

Success Check

• Match your setup and swing to the slope ___

To Increase Difficulty

• Make practice swings with your eyes closed.
• Practice hitting toward targets.
• Alternate shots with rear and target foot on the bucket.

To Decrease Difficulty

• Select either the uphill or downhill shot.
• Reduce total swings to 6.

a

Descending angle of approach

b

Ascending angle of approach

4. Cluster Drill

Distance and accuracy control in short shots can be affected by uneven lies. The back areas of practice greens and tees can provide good practice areas for these shots. Get permission and use whiffle balls.

a. Using a pitching wedge or 9-iron, practice the pitch shot from each type of uneven lie. Try to emphasize consistency in distance and direction, trying to group the balls within 8 to 10 yards of each other from about 25 yards away. Be sure to use your setup routine before each shot.

b. Using a 9- or 7-iron, practice the chip shot from each of the uneven lies. Hit balls for consistency in distance and direction. Be sure to use your setup routine before each shot.

Success Goal = 40 total shots, 20 chip shots and 20 pitch shots, from uneven lies with practice swings from flat lies

    a. 20 total pitch shots, alternating practice swings from a flat lie, grouping balls into 8- to 10-yard cluster

        3 pitches from uphill lie ____

        2 practice swings regular lie ____

        3 pitches from uphill lie ____

        3 pitches from downhill lie ____

        2 practice swings regular lie ____

        2 pitches from sidehill lie, balls below feet ____

        5 pitches from sidehill lie, balls above feet ____

    b. 20 total chip shots, grouping balls into 5-yard cluster

        5 chips from uphill lie ____

        5 chips from downhill lie ____

        5 chips from sidehill lie, balls below feet ____

        5 chips from sidehill lie, balls above feet ____

✔ Success Check

• Make practice swings to feel the slope ____
• Trust the feel of the practice swing ____

To Increase Difficulty

• Reduce target goal to within 5-yard clusters.
• Increase success goal to 70% of shots landing within 8 to 10 yards.

To Decrease Difficulty

• Practice either chip or pitch shot, not both.

Practice distance and accuracy control in short shots with the Cluster Drill.

UNEVEN LIE SUCCESS SUMMARY

Are you ready to play in Vermont, Austria, or Africa? Learning to adapt to a variety of lies allows you to have greater enjoyment—and less frustration—as you play throughout the country or world.

Be sure to consider the effects of the uneven lies as you play elevated greens. Though not as pronounced an influence on your swing, they can influence your shot results. Factoring in the uphill slope on your chip shot can make the difference in your "up and down" percentages.

Review your checklist in Figures 9.3 and 9.4 as you practice. Note the sidehill lies are more similar than different, and the uphill and downhill lies differ only in their setups to the full swing motion. Have a friend or teacher observe you. Have fun as you travel around the world of golf!

STEP 10

MENTAL CONTROL: FOCUSING AND LETTING GO

The game of golf requires not only the physical skills you have practiced in the previous sections but also mental skills to direct your body and allow it to execute the physical skills. Because golf requires both strength and precision, it is important that you learn to relax as you prepare to hit your golf shot and take advantage of the fact that each shot is a "contest" of its own—to put the ball where you want. This step provides you the opportunity to develop the skills to optimize your level of body tension to prepare for your best round of golf.

Each golf swing can be thought of as a separate, self-paced movement. Because you have complete control over when and how you hit the shot, what you do before you start your swing can be used as a solid base. Your preshot behaviors should be almost identical for each shot and serve as a reliable, and repeatable, first step. Your preparation routine should be practiced so much that it becomes an automatic part of each shot. You should go through it for each shot and especially when distracted or under pressure of competition.

If you do the same thing before each shot, you can check that you are ready for the swing and also be sure that your body is in the best position to act.

Your preswing routine, established in Step 2, allows you to focus your attention and get in the best position to hit the ball. It also helps keep you from being overanalytic. Some golfers find themselves thinking about the specifics of their shots or doubting their abilities just before hitting the ball. During the preshot routine, and practice swing, you can free your mind of all of those thoughts. Remember, as Jack Nicklaus said, "The golf swing happens far too fast for you to direct your muscles consciously—you must let it go."

In golf, a preshot routine should include selecting a target and club, concentrating, and taking your setup. You should select a sequence that makes you feel especially relaxed and comfortable. Your setup may be different from what someone else does. There is no one right sequence, just *your* sequence. The key to success is that you do the same things before each of your shots.

Why Is Mental Control Important?

When you watch great tennis players serve or basketball players shoot free throws, notice how they do the same thing before each shot. Some bounce the ball the same number of times before each attempt; others take a deep breath and spin the ball in their hands. These are not merely superstitious behaviors—they are part of the preshot preparation and serve as a signal to the body that it is time for action.

How to Establish Mental Control

Every golfer's mental control is mediated by his or her unique preshot routine. Though there are some common aspects of every good preshot routine, the order and some specific characteristics differ from golfer to golfer. For any one golfer, though, the aspects of the routine should always take place in the same order and take about the same amount of time for every shot.

Most preshot routines in golf consist of three steps:

1. selection of target and club,
2. self-monitoring of relaxation, tension control, concentration, and imagery, and
3. the physical aspects of the setup (as practiced in Step 2).

Because golf is a target game, one of the most important aspects of your preshot routine is to decide on the target and select the club. You can best do this by focusing on four things: LTD and target line. Determine the *lie* of the ball, the needed *trajectory* for the ball flight, the *distance* to the target, and then select the *target line*.

Your preshot routine will also help you control your attention and relax before each shot. If your shots don't always go where you want them to, the cause may be your swing or things in your mind that cause tension and get in the way of your swing. Practicing both the mental and physical aspects of your swing will greatly improve your score!

Tension Control

One of the biggest problems in golf is trying too hard. When you really want to hit a shot well, or when there is a small safe landing area and all you can see is the water hazard or the traps surrounding the green, you must be able to control your tension. If you are distracted by such challenges, you will probably hit poor shots because of the added tension, which can especially affect your hands, shoulders, and back. Imagine where your shot would go if you held onto your club like a hammer—a "white knuckle" or "gorilla grip." Some golfers perceive excess tension most at the end of a practice session or round of golf, when their hands feel achy or their shoulders tight. If you grip your club too tightly, you cannot release your hands through the area of impact with the ball; the result is a slice. How do we know that? Remember when you observed the ball flights in Step 4—we discussed the fact that when a ball curves as it flies through the air, it is because of the spin imparted to the ball due to the angle of the clubface at

contact with the ball. The most common result of too much tension is a slice, which occurs when the hands do not release and the face of the club is open.

It is important to learn to feel tension so you can control it before it controls the flight of your golf ball. In order to understand what happens when you are tense and to be able to feel when tension is a problem, practice this exercise: Imagine that the best, semi-relaxed grip on a golf club is a 3 on a scale of 1-5, a much too tight grip is a 5, and a very loose grip is a 1. Now hit a few golf balls using 5, 3, and 1 grips. (Just be careful that with a 1, you do not let the club fly out of your hands!) Compare the different feels and the results on the flight of your ball.

How to Control Tension

The keys to tension control (see Figure 10.1) are being able to keep your body in a balanced range of dynamic tension (around a 3 on our scale of 1-5) and detecting when it gets outside of that optimal range. If one part of your body is too tense (e.g., your hands or shoulders), you can learn to correct the tension level in much the same way that you corrected your slice or hook. When you find yourself with excess tension or negative thoughts, take a deep breath and exhale fully. This physiological mechanism signals your body that you are in control.

A technique called *progressive relaxation* takes advantage of the same principle of "playing in the extremes to find the means" that you practiced before. Start by tensing your muscles to the maximum (5), then relax them completely (1). Then find the medium level of tension at 3.

Try it. Make a very tight fist with both hands (5) and then take a big deep breath. Now exhale fully and release the tension in your hands to a 1 level. This deep breath technique is a very powerful signal to your body and can become a good method for you to use. Whenever you feel tense, take a deep breath, exhale, and then regain control to the medium level of 3.

FIGURE
10.1

KEYS TO SUCCESS

TENSION CONTROL

1. Do a quick check of tension. Strive for an "optimal 3"
   a. Neck and shoulders ____
   b. Hands (grip) ____
   c. Back ____
   d. Legs ____
2. Selective relaxation
   a. Take a deep breath ____
   b. Exhale fully and smile to relax your face ____
   c. If too tight, go to a 5, and then relax down to a 4, and then the optimal 3 ____
3. Recheck tension
   a. 3 in neck and shoulders ____
   b. 3 in back ____
   c. 3 in legs ____
   d. 3 in hands (grip) ____

It requires self-monitoring to detect body tension, relax your body to its optimal level, and focus on the swing itself. You must learn to "let go" and allow your body to automatically "run off" each swing without interference from distracting thoughts or influences. Train your body and then trust it.

Why Is Concentration Important?

Distracting thoughts may be related to many different things, including loud noises, thoughts about previous shots missed, daydreams about future shots, anger at yourself for a mistake, or concern over what someone else might be thinking about you or the unrequested advice they are giving. Sometimes distracting thoughts involve things unrelated to your golf game such as a problem at work, where to eat dinner, or how to deal with a family concern. None of those thoughts can help with the shot you are about to hit. Instead, you should think only about the shot at hand.

It never helps to worry about what might have been if only you had practiced harder, or if you had hit an earlier shot better. Nor does it help to daydream about what might come true (see Figure 10.2). Instead, focus on what you are doing, decide what shot to hit,

"One more great shot and I'll win!"

Figure 10.2 Daydreaming about future shots distracts your concentration.

and then relax and let your skills run off automatically.

Another time you lose concentration is when you get angry. When that happens tension increases and your attention shifts. Many golfers seem to feel that a little anger is all right, but only if it allows you to concentrate more and boosts your energy. As Tom Kite has said, "A little bit of anger means you care and are going to play harder, to pay more attention. Uncontrolled anger means you're going to ruin your round."

Here are a few ways to control anger and tension:

- Thought stoppage combined with positive thoughts
- Controlling tension by "choking" your putter (to a 5 level) and then letting go (and returning to the 3 level of optimal tension)
- Taking a deep breath and blowing out the anger

If you find that you are getting angry or thinking nonproductive thoughts, stop these thoughts by using the *thought stoppage* technique. The first step is to recognize the negative or undermining thoughts; then immediately stop them and replace them with self-enhancing, affirming thoughts (see Figure 10.3).

Most great golfers acknowledge that they talk to themselves. The key is that they talk confidently and do not second-guess themselves. For example, Greg Norman is well known for his positive self-talk. Says Norman:

"The tougher the shot I'm facing, the more I talk [to myself]. If I'm on the last hole of a tournament and concerned about a shot, I say to myself, "You know this shot cold, you've knocked it stiff a thousand times, and now you're going to do it again.""

If you don't use self-talk to build confidence, it may work against you. If you say, "Oh no . . . look at that water!" or "How could I be so dumb? A double bogie got me here," you may be building negative feelings and tension.

If your thoughts do not always go where you want them to, the cause may be your swing or things in your mind that cause tension and get in the way of your swing. One of your biggest problems may be that you are trying too hard.

Use the Keys to Success (Figure 10.4) to check your mental preparation.

The key to great golf is training and trusting your

Figure 10.3 An example of the thought stoppage technique.

FIGURE
10.4  **KEYS TO SUCCESS**

CONCENTRATION

a

b

c

Focus Thoughts

1. Set down bag as signal to focus in ___
2. Check for any negative thoughts/emotions or lack of concentration ___
3. Identify the specific negative thoughts/emotions or lack of concentration ___

Thought Stoppage

1. Use trigger to abruptly stop negative thought (snap fingers, slap thigh, etc.) ___
2. Take deep breath ___
3. Exhale to regain control and blow out self-doubts ___
4. Make positive statement ___
5. Refocus on present ___
6. Initiate preshot routine ___

Preshot Routine

1. Select target ___
2. Select club ___
3. Grip club while standing behind ball ___
4. Choose intermediate target ___
5. Take practice swing ___
6. Align clubface ___
7. Set feet and get comfortable ___
8. Check target ___
9. Check tension (3 level all over) ___
10. Focus in and let go ___
11. Clear thoughts (use swing cue) ___

SUCCESS STOPPERS FOR MENTAL CONTROL

The flight of your golf ball can tell you a great deal about both your physical performance and your mental approach to golf. As was discussed in Step 4, the flight of your ball can be used to detect many problems with your golf swing. The flight of your golf ball is affected not only directly by your physical swing but also indirectly by mental processes influencing your physical technique. If mental tension causes you to grip your club too tightly, you cannot release your hand through the area of impact with the ball—a slice results. Similarly, if you constantly top the ball, it may be because of too much tension in your shoulders, which could be alleviated by conscious relaxation. The errors listed below represent the most common problems related to tension control.

ERROR	CORRECTION
1. You have too much tension on backswing, causing you to extend your trunk, stand too tall, and top the ball.	1. Keep arms and back at medium tension (level 3).
2. Grip is too loose at top, causing collapse at ball or hitting ground behind ball.	2. Keep grip at desired level of tension (3) throughout swing
3. You have too much tension in shoulders, causing you to top the ball.	3. Keep shoulders at optimal level (3).
4. Lower body and legs give in (flex), causing club to hit ground behind ball.	4. Keep posture at optimal tension level (3).
5. When standing on tee overlooking water hazard, thoughts focus on possible lost ball; when driven, sure enough—ball goes into water.	5. Think about and see safe landing areas, not possible problem; imagine ball landing safely. Use self-talk to replace negative thoughts.
6. You think about great round you are playing, then whiff ball.	6. Focus on present shot; use entire routine and swing cue "smooth."
7. You think about past problems hitting out of bunkers, doubt your ability, then miss shots on the course that you hit well in practice.	7. Use thought stoppage; say, "I have done this 50 times in practice, and I know I can do it now."

MENTAL CONTROL

DRILLS

1. Tension Control Drill

Imagine that the tension possible in different body parts ranges from 1 to 5, with 3 being perfect for you. Systematically vary the tension in your shoulders, hands (grip), back, legs. For example, set the tension in your grip at 1 and hit 2 shots, then switch to a 5 and hit 2 shots.

Hit two shots at each tension level (1, 5, 3) in each isolated body part, while maintaining an optimal 3 in all other body parts. Notice what happens to the ball flight for each change in tension (see Figures a-c).

Success Goal = 24 total shots, varying tension

    6 shots with shoulder tension (1, 5, and 3): 2 shots at each level _____

    6 shots with grip tension (1, 5, and 3): 2 shots at each level _____

    6 shots with tension in back (1, 5, and 3): 2 shots at each level _____

    6 shots with tension in legs (1, 5, and 3): 2 shots at each level _____

To Increase Difficulty

• Partners specify tension in each body part (e.g., 5 in rear hand, 1 in target hand, and 2 in shoulders).

To Decrease Difficulty

• Execute shots while experiencing tension in an ascending order of tension (from 1 to 5).

Success Check

• Check body tension before each shot _____
• Adjust tension to your optimal "3" level _____

a
Loose grip (tension level 1) causes you to hit ground behind ball.

b
Tight grip (tension level 5) causes you to top ball.

c
Grip at desired level of tension (3).

2. Partner Distraction Drill

Working with a partner, take turns taking shots while the other says distracting things or tosses paper, tees, or grass into the shooter's visual field. Being able to adjust to and ignore such distractions is good concentration practice. Using a 5-iron, hit 10 balls toward a selected target, using your routine each time.

Success Goal = hitting 10 balls with entire routine, maintaining concentration in spite of partner's attempts to distract ____

Success Check

• Use routine consistently, maintain focus and concentration ____

To Increase Difficulty

• Work in groups of 3-4, with one person hitting and all others attempting to distract.

To Decrease Difficulty

• Limit the number of distraction tactics used at a time.

3. Circle Alignment Drill Without Routine

To appreciate the value of your routine, try hitting 10 balls without using your routine. Walk up to the ball, walk around it twice, count backward by 3, take your setup, aim at a target, and swing. Noticing where the ball lands, set your club on the ground along your toes and walk back to check how close your alignment was to the desired target line. Notice whether you tend to aim to the right or left of the desired target; this is your *bias*. (Note: The club will not point directly at the target; it should be parallel to your target line.)

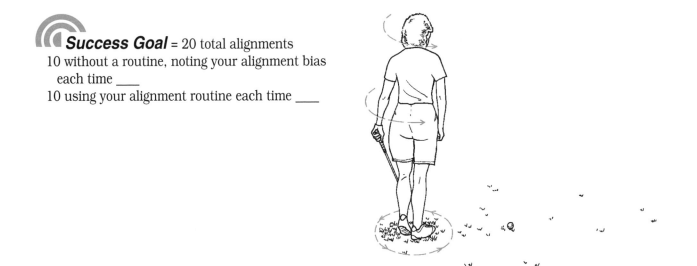

Success Goal = 20 total alignments
10 without a routine, noting your alignment bias
   each time ____
10 using your alignment routine each time ____

After each shot, lay your club down across your toes and note whether there is an alignment bias to right or to left, and where the ball landed relative to the target.

Shot	Alignment Bias (Right, Left, or Target)	Ball Flight Bias (Right, Left, or Target)
1.		
2.		
3.		
4.		
5.		
6.		
7.		
8.		
9.		
10.		

4. Alignment Drill With Routine

Using routine each time, check whether alignment and ball flight were on target or with a bias

Shot	Alignment Bias	Ball Flight Bias
1.		
2.		
3.		
4.		
5.		
6.		
7.		
8.		
9.		
10.		

Success Check

• Check alignment carefully before each shot. When practicing, choose a different target each time and check alignment ____

To Increase Difficulty

• Change targets each time.
• After aligning to one target, change targets and reestablish alignment.

To Decrease Difficulty

• Leave the alignment club on the ground for 2 or 3 shots. Then choose a new target.

5. Possibilities Drill

While standing on the practice tee, imagine an actual hole from a golf course. State a self-doubting thought, *stop*, use thought stoppage to replace the thought with a good one related to safe landing areas, and then execute your routine.

Success Goal =

a. Imagine a large water hazard and a negative thought about your ability to hit over it (see Figure a, next page). Stop this thought, replace it with a good thought, then hit a ball over the imaginary water (see Figure b) ____

b. Imagine landing next to a sand trap and being afraid that your next shot would land in it. Stop this thought, replace it with a good one, and hit a ball over the imaginary trap ____

c. Imagine hitting a ball out of bounds and having to play a provisional ball from the same spot. Tell yourself that you can "never make this shot." Stop this thought, replace it with a positive thought, and hit a ball in play ____

d. Make up your own negative situation and practice positive thoughts about it ____

Success Check

• Use thought stoppage to replace negative thoughts with positive thoughts and images ____

To Increase Difficulty

• Have a partner create situations for you.

To Decrease Difficulty

• Record negative thoughts into a tape recorder and play them during practice.
• Use thought stoppage after each negative thought to replace it with a positive thought.

a   Negative possibility

b   Positive possibility

6. Distraction Drill

Try forcing yourself to think about other things while hitting golf balls. Hit 5 shots each while (a) counting backward from 100 by 3s, (b) humming or singing a song (quietly), and (c) reciting poetry. Observe what happens to the flight of the ball.

Success Goal = 15 shots while talking to yourself

   5 shots while counting backward from 100 by 3s ____

   5 shots while humming or singing a song ____

   5 shots while reciting a poem or saying the alphabet backward ____

"100, 97, 94, 91, 88, 85, 82, 79, 76"

Success Check
• Check body tension and readjust to 3 ____
• Observe ball flights ____

To Increase Difficulty
- Have a partner distract you with random talk.
- Have partner criticize your game.

To Decrease Difficulty
- Hum or use nonverbal distraction.
- Clear mind before hitting.

7. Positive Self-Talk Drill

Everyone talks to himself/herself. This language of the mind can have a tremendous influence on performance—working to help when the thoughts are positive and goal directed, or working against you when thoughts are negative or self-defeating. When negative thoughts occur, replace them with positive, self-enhancing thoughts by using the thought stoppage technique.

On a piece of paper, write down self-defeating thoughts, and then add options that are self-enhancing.

Self-Defeating Thought	**Self-Enhancing Thought**
1. _____	_____
2. _____	_____
3. _____	_____
4. _____	_____
5. _____	_____

Success Goal =

a. Write down five negative thoughts you've had while practicing or playing golf (e.g., "I can't ever seem to hit a 5-wood") and then replace the thought with a positive one, such as "If I take my time, I know I can hit a good shot," or "I will use my preshot routine just the way I have been practicing it, and then I'll hit it straight."

a. Rephrase negative, counterproductive statements to emphasize positive, or self-enhancing statements _____

b. Make an audio tape or script of a series of negative thoughts, which are then countered by positive thoughts _____

Success Check

- Recognize counterproductive or negative thoughts _____
- Interrupt negative thought and replace it with a positive self-enhancing thought _____

To Decrease Difficulty

- Make an audio tape or script of the toughest negative thoughts and practice changing them to positive or self-enhancing thoughts.
- Use a tape recorder to tape all of the thoughts that occur during practice or play.

a Self-defeating thought   b Self-enhancing thought

MENTAL CONTROL SUCCESS SUMMARY

The key to great golf is training and trusting your body. Practice (train) carefully and then "get out of the way" of your swing and trust yourself. A consistent and repeatable preshot routine allows you to start each swing in the same way. It makes it much easier to be relaxed and focused, to build confidence, and to hit the shot. Ask a partner or friend to check whether your mental preparation is helping or hurting your game by using the checklists in Figures 10.1 and 10.4.

Also complete the following self-test on mental control. Respond to each statement in terms of whether you strongly agree (**SA**), agree (**A**), disagree (**D**), or strongly disagree (**SD**).

1. When I play golf, I have a great deal of tension in my
   a. neck and shoulders   **SA A D SD**
   b. hands (grip)   **SA A D SD**
   c. back   **SA A D SD**
   d. legs   **SA A D SD**
2. I use my preshot routine before each shot.   **SA A D SD**
3. I have a specific cue to regain attention when I approach my next shot.   **SA A D SD**
4. I always take my grip on the club from the same relative spot.   **SA A D SD**
5. I use an intermediate target to aid in alignment.   **SA A D SD**
6. I always align the clubface with the target line.   **SA A D SD**
7. If I detect too much tension or too little, I always walk away and begin my preshot routine again.   **SA A D SD**
8. I can relax and reestablish tension control if I detect too much or too little tension.
   SA A D SD
9. After I hit a shot, I take time to remember how it felt and learn from it.   **SA A D SD**
10. After a round of golf, I am willing to let go of the ineffective shots and tension, and store away the good shots.   **SA A D SD**

SHOT SELECTION AND COURSE MANAGEMENT: BECOMING A THINKING PLAYER

E ffective course management is essential if you are to use your skills to shoot low numbers on the links. In this step you will learn how to plan the best strategy to play each hole. When combined with the skills you developed in Steps 3 through 10, you will have the best chance to become a great golfer. Good course management allows you to apply your skills to go from the tee to the green in the fewest number of strokes, no matter what the situation—narrow fairways, dog-legs, deep traps, water hazards, and so forth. This step helps you develop your game strategy by presenting a three-step approach (AIP: assess, identify, and plot) to course management.

Why Is Course Management Important?

Can you imagine a coach preparing for a game without a game plan? Just as a coach matches players' strengths against the weaknesses of the other team, you must match up your skills with the golf course's characteristics. Your ability to analyze the strengths and weaknesses of a hole, along with the knowledge of your current golf ability, helps you develop a strategy for course management by carefully analyzing each hole and selecting your best route to the green. Through course management, you match your strengths as a player against the weaknesses of each hole you play. This is "percentage golf" and is important in becoming a consistent player because it puts you in control of your game.

How to Select Shots and Manage the Course

Course management is the real challenge in golf. Many golfers are good practice players because there are no consequences. The conditions in practice remain the same, and it is easy not to have to make many decisions. To become a good player, though, you must learn to think yourself around the course. Use the *AIP* course-management strategy: *assess* your current strengths and weaknesses as a player, *identify* the strengths and weaknesses of the specific golf hole you are about to play, and plan the best strategy by *plotting* a route to the green, given these considerations.

The first step in course management is to *assess* your own strengths and weaknesses as a player. When you practice and play, use the drills that were presented with each step to help you in this assessment. How close do you come to the Success Goals? When you use the charts to record your ball flights, do you have any biases in your shots? For example, do you tend to hit more balls to the right or left of your target with your irons or woods? Do you tend to hit more chip shots long, short, or on target? Step 12: The 19th Hole, provides a systematic way to develop an awareness of your strengths and weaknesses, and plan for progress.

The second step in effective course management is to *identify* the strengths and weaknesses of each hole. The tough things about a hole are referred to as the hole's *strengths*. Strengths include such things as the hazards (water and sand), out-of-bounds areas, small fairways and greens, dog-legs, and high roughs. Most holes have specific strengths that were designed by the golf course architect to give the golfer trouble. On the other hand, there are weaknesses in most holes, which should tell you where to aim. For example, find the widest part of the fairway, aim away from the hazards, look for an opening to the green where there are no traps, find the largest part of the green to aim at rather than always aiming at the flag (see Figure 11.1).

The identification of a hole's strengths and weaknesses can often take place from the tee. Carefully look at the entire hole. Where are the weaknesses of the hole? Where are the strengths? Are there any distinguishable yardage markers? For some holes, you may not be able to see the entire hole from the tee. Often the scorecard has a printed layout of the course with yardage marked, or one of your playing partners may be familiar with the course.

The third step is to compare your strengths to the weaknesses of the hole and *plot* a path or route to the green. For example, standing on the tee, look first at both the strengths and weaknesses of the hole. If you see a sand trap on the right side, you probably want to select a landing area on the left side of the fairway. By determining a good strategy, you avoid the trouble built into the course and take advantage of the good landing areas. This strategy will then dictate the clubs you choose to hit (see Figure 11.2).

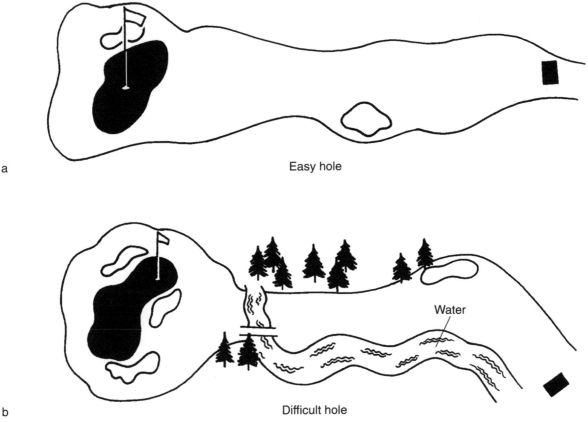

a   Easy hole

b   Difficult hole

Figure 11.1 Potential trouble areas determine the strengths of a hole, ranging from few trouble areas (a) to many trouble areas (b).

**FIGURE
11.2**

KEYS TO SUCCESS

COURSE MANAGEMENT:
ASSESS, IDENTIFY, AND PLOT

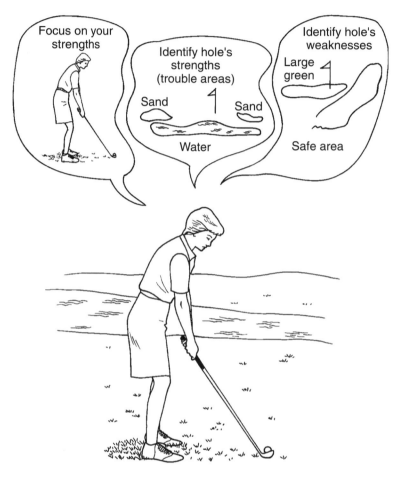

Assess Your Strengths

1. Control of ball direction ____
2. Ball trajectory per club____
3. Distance hit per club____
4. Ball curvature tendencies (slice and hook) ____
5. Psychological characteristics and mental control ____
6. Tension control ____
7. Concentration ____

Identify Hole's Strengths and Weaknesses

1. Hazards (water/sand) ___
2. Out-of-bounds ____
3. Tight fairway ____
4. Small green ____
5. Narrow opening to green ____
6. High rough ____
7. Trees and shrubs ____

Plot a Route

1. Locate safe landing areas, as opposed to hazards or other trouble ___
2. Consider width of fairway (tight or open) ___
3. Consider location and height of rough ___
4. Find opening to green (free of hazards) ___
5. Select appropriate clubs
   a. Lie of ball ___
   b. Trajectory of desired shot ___
   c. Distance ball must travel ___

Your club selection is based on the position or lie of the ball, the trajectory of the shot, and the desired distance to your target or landing area. Each of these aspects is important to the golfer, and are sometimes referred to as the *LTD* process: the *lie* of the ball, the needed *trajectory*, and the desired *distance*. The *lie* of the ball is determined by its position in the sand, grass, divot, or on a bare spot. For example, is the ball on top of the grass or sand or resting in a divot, buried in the sand, or on a hill? The lie can also be influenced by the height or texture of the grass.

Ideal shot *trajectory* is a matter of how high or low you wish to hit the shot. Is the normal trajectory for a particular club adequate? Are there trees or shrubs to go over? Do you need to stop the ball quickly?

The *distance* is determined by how far you wish to hit this shot and the next shot. It is important to remember that it is not always necessary to hit the ball as far as you possibly can. Sometimes you wish to hit a controlled, shorter distance in order to be in a good position to hit your next shot. For example, if there is a water hazard in front of the green and you are 190 yards away, you may wish to hit short of the water and then hit your next shot onto the green.

Your club selection ultimately must depend on all three elements of LTD—lie, trajectory, and distance. For example, a wood is not recommended from high grass, yet the distance might naturally call for that club. In such a case, an iron might become the preferred club because of the grassy conditions.

COURSE MANAGEMENT SUCCESS STOPPERS

Many of the problems in course management come from not taking the time to make good decisions. Outstanding golfers allow themselves time to analyze the situation and match each hole's demands with their skills. They use the AIP strategy of assessing, identifying, and plotting.

ERROR	CORRECTION
1. Ball generally lands short of green when you use 4-iron.	1. Take "one more club" than you think; that is, if you believe you should hit with a 4-iron, choose a 5-wood or 3-iron.
2. Tee shots usually miss fairway.	2. Tee off with a 5-wood or long iron.
3. When you try to hook ball around dog-leg, ball ends up in woods.	3. Play for middle of fairway, particularly if you tend to slice.
4. When there is a lateral water hazard on hole, ball always seems to land there.	4. Use tension control to feel level-3 grip. Be sure to use routine and focus on the good landing areas rather than being distracted by water.

COURSE MANAGEMENT

DRILLS

1. Imaginary Hole Drill

It is important to be able to match your strengths and weaknesses with those of a golf hole. To begin practicing this skill, imagine that you are on the first tee of a golf course, though you're actually on a practice tee. Determine the desired landing area in an open space. Use the obstacles or flags in the field to represent "trouble" on the hole. Select the safe landing areas and then actually hit a shot toward each one.

Success Goal = choose 10 different safe landing areas, hit 1 ball to each target area, and have balls land in safe areas 8 of 10 times

Shot	Landing area	Club used	Result
Example	Between blue flag and orange cone	5-iron	Good shot, slightly long
1			
2			
3			
4			
5			
6			
7			
8			
9			
10			

Success Check

• Determine the strengths (trouble) of the hole ____
• Match hole's weaknesses with your strengths ____

To Increase Difficulty

• Mark actual "trouble areas" in practice area.
• Increase the number/size of hole's strengths (trouble areas).

2. Alternate Strategies

In your mind, create an imaginary hole. Imagine that each obstacle in your practice field is a hazard or trouble spot on a real hole. For example, pretend that the area between two flags or cones is really a lake. Find a landing area away from that "water hazard."

Pretend you are three different golfers, with different characteristic strengths and weaknesses. As each golfer, determine a different strategy for playing the hole. Identify the safe landing area, and choose the club to be used for your first shot. As golfer #1, assume that you are a long hitter with a good short game. What landing area would you choose, and what club would you hit? As golfer #2, assume that you hit short and tend to slice the ball. Golfer #3 is really you. Describe yourself and determine your preferred route.

Success Goal = plan a route for three types of golfers:
1) long hitter with good short game;
2) short hitter who tends to slice; and
3) yourself.

Diagram the selected landing area, route, and actual outcome. Specify the club used, and hit the shot.

<u>**As golfer #1**</u>   <u>**As golfer #2**</u>   <u>**As golfer #3**</u>

Success Check
- Determine strengths (trouble) of the hole _____
- Match hole's weaknesses with your strengths _____

To Increase or Decrease Difficulty
- Have partner make up or adjust the characteristics of the hole.
- Have partner describe a fictitious golfer and match those strengths to hole's weakness.

3. Listing Strengths and Weaknesses Drill

Given the sample of three golf holes (see Figures a-c under the Success Goal), identify the strengths and weaknesses of the holes. Write a brief description of each and mark their locations on the diagram. Mark each hole's strengths as s1, s2, and s3; indicate the locations of the weaknesses as w1, w2, w3 (see example hole).

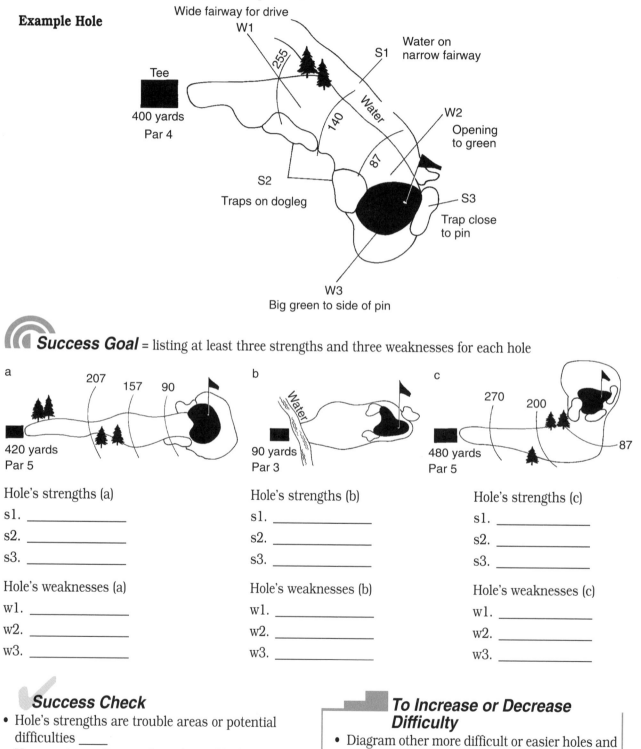

Example Hole

Wide fairway for drive
W1

Water on narrow fairway
S1

Tee
400 yards
Par 4

255

140

Water

87

W2
Opening to green

S2
Traps on dogleg

S3
Trap close to pin

W3
Big green to side of pin

Success Goal = listing at least three strengths and three weaknesses for each hole

a
207 157 90
420 yards
Par 5

b
Water
90 yards
Par 3

c
270 200
480 yards
Par 5
87

Hole's strengths (a)
s1. _____
s2. _____
s3. _____

Hole's strengths (b)
s1. _____
s2. _____
s3. _____

Hole's strengths (c)
s1. _____
s2. _____
s3. _____

Hole's weaknesses (a)
w1. _____
w2. _____
w3. _____

Hole's weaknesses (b)
w1. _____
w2. _____
w3. _____

Hole's weaknesses (c)
w1. _____
w2. _____
w3. _____

✔ Success Check

• Hole's strengths are trouble areas or potential difficulties _____
• Have partners diagram hypothetical holes _____

To Increase or Decrease Difficulty

• Diagram other more difficult or easier holes and analyze them.

4. Managing an Entire Hole Drill

When you plan a strategy for a given hole, you must match your strengths as a golfer with the weaknesses of the hole. Identify your preferred landing area for each shot by marking an X over the spot. Indicate the club you should use to hit the ball from that location by placing a symbol adjacent to the X (e.g., 4i = 4-iron; 3w = 3-wood; pw = pitching wedge). See the example hole below.

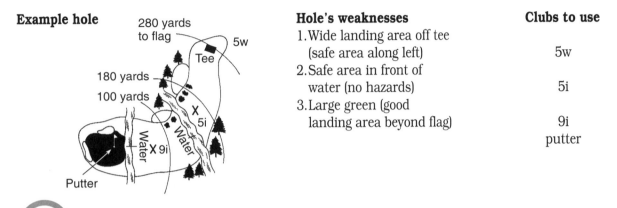

Example hole

Hole's weaknesses	Clubs to use
1. Wide landing area off tee (safe area along left)	5w
2. Safe area in front of water (no hazards)	5i
3. Large green (good landing area beyond flag)	9i putter

Success Goal = identify each hole's weaknesses, plot all shots for each hole, and indicate the clubs to use

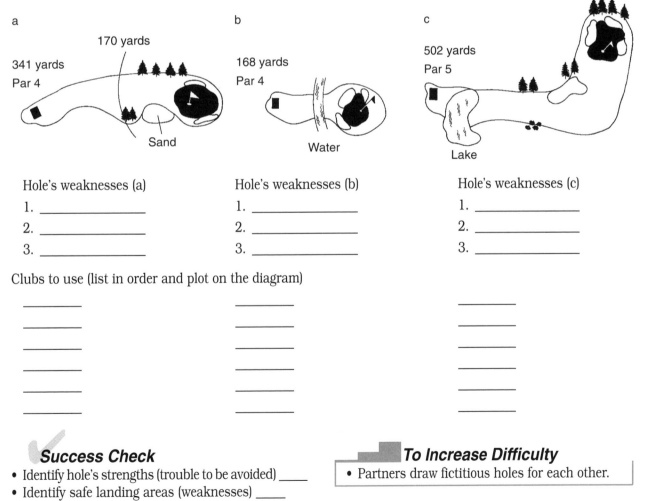

a

341 yards
Par 4
170 yards
Sand

b

168 yards
Par 4
Water

c

502 yards
Par 5
Lake

Hole's weaknesses (a)

1. _____
2. _____
3. _____

Hole's weaknesses (b)

1. _____
2. _____
3. _____

Hole's weaknesses (c)

1. _____
2. _____
3. _____

Clubs to use (list in order and plot on the diagram)

_____	_____	_____
_____	_____	_____
_____	_____	_____
_____	_____	_____
_____	_____	_____
_____	_____	_____

Success Check

• Identify hole's strengths (trouble to be avoided) ____
• Identify safe landing areas (weaknesses) ____

To Increase Difficulty

• Partners draw fictitious holes for each other.

5. Managing a Round Drill

Ultimately, the task in golf is to plot your strategy for a round of golf. Get the course diagram from a local or famous course layout, and determine how you would ideally play each hole, given your strengths and weaknesses. Lay out the shots you would make on each hole. Mark an X on the landing area and indicate the club you should hit from each location. If possible, actually play the course and keep track of your planned strategy compared to what actually happens.

Success Goal = plan your course management for each of 18 holes by plotting on a diagram

Success Check
- Identify holes' strengths (to be avoided) ____
- Focus on holes' weaknesses and match them to your strengths ____

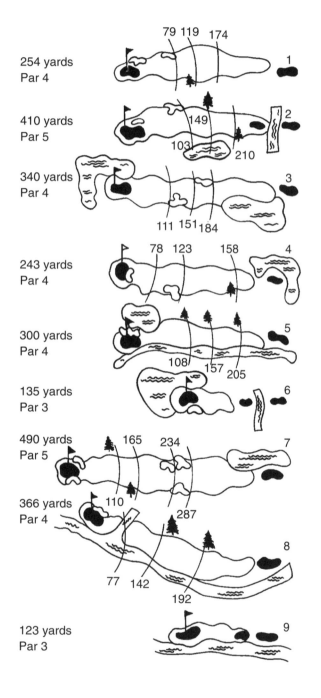

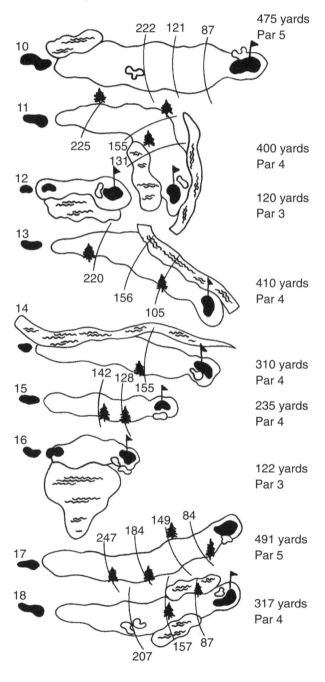

COURSE MANAGEMENT SUCCESS SUMMARY

In determining your ability to match your skills (strengths) against the weaknesses of a golf hole, use the 3-step AIP approach: *assess, identify,* and *plot* your best path to the green for each hole. When you actually play a round, plan the strategy for the entire round, and before teeing off on each hole, check it. If your plan needs to be changed after any shot, do so—but always stop to replan and refocus before hitting the next shot. Use the checklist in Figure 11.2 to be sure you are carefully planning. Place a check on the line for each element you consider when you attempt to determine your strategy for each hole.

STEP

12

THE 19TH HOLE: POSTROUND TIPS AND PRACTICE STRATEGIES

Whenever you hit a golf ball, you can learn something about your swing. In Step 4, you learned to watch the flight of your ball in order to identify your strengths and to detect basic problems with your golf swing. This technique can help you on the practice tee and the course, but you need other skills to help detect your strengths and weaknesses from a regulation round of golf.

When you play golf, you almost never use the same club twice in a row. Because of the constant demands to match the requirements of shots, it is easy to lose track of just how well you are doing. This step provides you with several techniques to help you systematically identify your strengths and weaknesses during a round of golf and plan a strategy for effective practice. Remember that it is essential to systematically practice—"failing to plan and practice is planning to fail."

Why Is Learning From Your Round of Golf Important?

Some golfers are very good practice players and seem to hit many excellent shots in practice, but they do not play well when they attempt an actual round of golf. A round of golf should be used just like practice—to learn more about yourself and your golf game, including both mental and physical aspects. Great golfers spend time after each round focusing on what they did and how they thought or felt in order to learn more about their skills, and direct their future practice.

How to Learn From a Round of Golf

During each round of golf you try to hit your best shot each time you strike a ball. When you hit a good shot, remember how you prepared to hit it and how it felt during the swing (replay the good). Of course, it is not always possible to hit great shots, so it is also important to try to determine what went wrong when you mis-hit a ball and consider how you would do it differently next time (replace the bad). Pay attention to the ball flight outcomes and to your mental preparation to hit the ball and the physical aspects of your swing.

In golf, the competitive situation involves an actual round of golf in which you can test your skills and abilities. During a round, you may use every club in your bag and hit 100 or more shots. This experience should provide a wealth of information about your golf skill, if you are systematic about keeping track of your performance. It is important to pay attention to how well you execute each swing. Just like a basketball player might keep track of the position on the floor from which he or she shot, you should keep track of the golf clubs and shots you use. Your tracking system should include both the physical outcome of your swings and your psychological characteristics and control for each shot during the round.

After each shot, focus on what happened to the ball. Determine what might have caused any problems. *What were the physical characteristics of the shot and resultant ball flight?* What was the ball flight? Was it on line with the target? Was there excessive curve in the ball flight (a slice or hook)? What was the trajectory? Was the distance the shot traveled about right for that particular club? Were there problems with alignment, the path of the swing (causing a push or pull), topping or popping up the ball, or selecting a club—problems that resulted in a shot that was too short or too long in relation to the desired target?

Shot Mapping

One excellent way to learn from a round of golf is to keep track of each shot you hit. By actually drawing each golf hole (or using the diagram on the scorecard), it is easy to record the shots that you hit. This *shot mapping* technique is a very convenient way to be

able to remember what shots you took and how well you executed them. Figure 12.1 illustrates a chart of 9 holes of golf. Notice that for each hole, the club that was used as well as a note about the results are recorded.

Shotkeeper Scorecard

The result of each golf ball you hit is affected by two shot aspects: your (1) physical swing and (2) mental state when you hit the ball. The errors that result from psychological skills are not as easy to detect as physical skills. You cannot see them, and no one else can see them to tell you about them. You must be the detective; be sensitive to your own body and mind and record what happened. When you hit the last shot, were you tense, distracted, rushed, unable to concentrate? Record any of these feelings so that you can practice good mental skills just like you practice the physical aspects of your game.

The Shotkeeper Scorecard (see Figure 12.2) enables

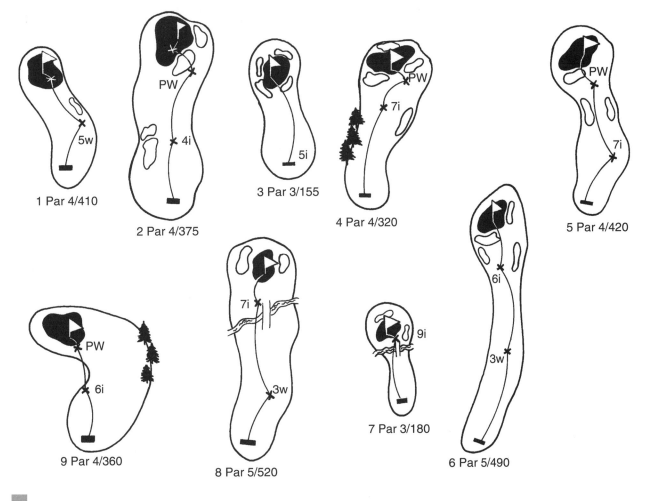

1 Par 4/410

2 Par 4/375

3 Par 3/155

4 Par 4/320

5 Par 4/420

6 Par 5/490

7 Par 3/180

8 Par 5/520

9 Par 4/360

Figure 12.1 Sample of Shot Mapping.

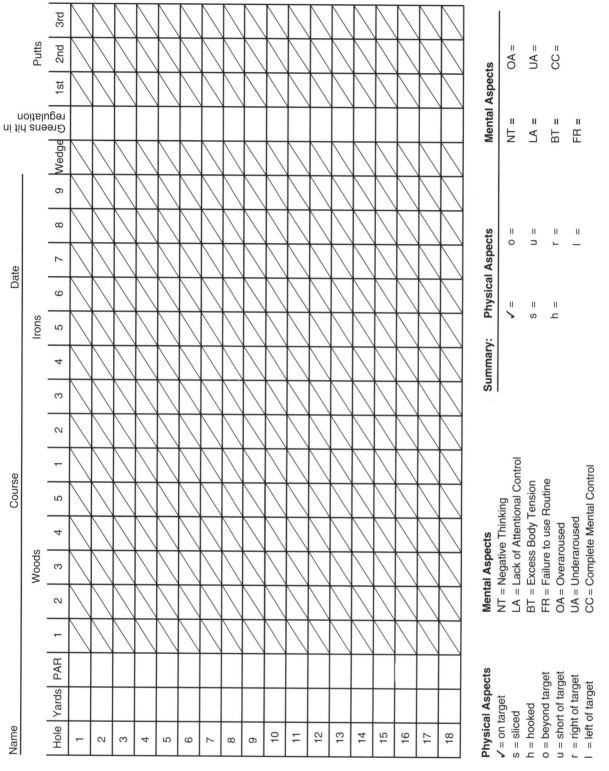

Physical Aspects
✓ = on target
s = sliced
h = hooked
o = beyond target
u = short of target
r = right of target
l = left of target

Mental Aspects
NT = Negative Thinking
LA = Lack of Attentional Control
BT = Excess Body Tension
FR = Failure to use Routine
OA = Overaroused
UA = Underaroused
CC = Complete Mental Control

Note: From Golf: Better Practice for Better Play by L. Bunker & D. Owens, 1984, p. 210. Copyright 1984 by Leisure Press. Adapted by permission.

Figure 12.2 Shotkeeper Scorecard.

you to learn from your round of golf by allowing you to record each shot you take. This lets you systematically collect data on each of the clubs in your bag and on your mental and physical skills. The scorecard allows you to record two items for each club used: notations about the physical results of the shot and the mental skills you demonstrated. A blank scorecard for you to copy and use appears in the Appendix (p. 159).

In the sample Shotkeeper Scorecard that Tony completed, notice the tendencies tallied on the scoresheet (see Figure 12.3). There were 9 slices, compared to only 1 hook. There were also 23 instances of having excess body tension, whereas only once was underarousal (being too relaxed) a problem. From this example it is easy to see that one problem for Tony may be tension, preventing the return of the clubface to a square position at impact. This tendency to be too aroused often causes an open clubface, which results in slicing the ball. As a result of this self-analysis Tony will go to step 10 and focus the practice session on tension control and "letting go."

Planning Effective Practice

Effective practice in golf requires that you systematically work to make the fundamental skills automatic and then learn to apply them in many different situations. An integrated approach to golf means that you must take what you have learned in the preceding steps of this book, practice those skills individually, and then create sequences similar to those you experience on the golf course. This step focuses on combining your technique practice with the information you learned from playing each round of golf.

Why Is Effective Practice Important?

Golf is different from many other sports due to the individual shots that you execute at your own pace. You are not required to respond to the pace of a moving object or to react to another player's motions. However, you must be able to respond to the various environmental situations that occur in golf, such as various ball lies, preferred trajectories, distances to targets, and irregular terrain. Therefore, during practice you should practice isolated techniques as well as the variations that can occur on the golf course. You have been provided knowledge and practice strategies for each skill in the preceding steps to success. It is possible to practice almost every conceivable shot including putting during practice, so why not take advantage of this opportunity?

How to Effectively Practice Woods and Irons

The first few minutes of every practice should always be spent preparing your body for success. Before each practice, be sure to go through the warm-up process discussed in the first section of this book. Remember to stretch slowly and to hold the stretch for a count of 15—do not bounce (see Figure 12.4a). Systematically work all of your body parts, focusing on flexibility. This helps you feel the stretch of your muscles and be ready to "tune in" to your body during practice.

Every practice session should start under the best conditions possible. Find a nice grassy area and practice your best shots. This allows you to build confidence as you develop a smooth, repeatable swing, which can be adapted to special course circumstances. Start your practice with the mid-irons first, then short irons, and clear target lines so that your alignment is the same for all shots (see Figure 12.4b). With each practice stroke, determine your target, focus on your posture and smooth swing, and watch the ball flight. Remember to use your preshot routine and check for good mental control.

Start your practice on the tee by placing a club on the ground pointing toward a target. Remember—golf is a target game, and you must have a target each time you swing in order to learn from the flight of your golf ball (see Figure 12.4c). In the beginning, always put your ball on a tee about half an inch above the ground when practicing the full swing to assure consistent ball lie as you develop your swing techniques. When you have achieved 50% consistency in ball flight during practice with your ball on a tee, alternate 3 swings with the tee and 2 swings with the ball on the ground. As you hit the ball, watch the ball flight. Use the feedback from each ball flight to check your basic skills (see Step 4 for a review). Effective practice keys are presented in Figure 12.4.

Performance Chart

Name: Tony Jones Course: Richmont CC Date: Sept. 9

Hole	Yards	PAR	Woods 1	Woods 2	Woods 3	Woods 4	Woods 5	Irons 1	Irons 2	Irons 3	Irons 4	Irons 5	Irons 6	Irons 7	Irons 8	Irons 9	Wedge	Greens hit in regulation	Putts 1st	Putts 2nd	Putts 3rd
1	385	4			s/BT							s/BT		s/BT			–/BT		u/CC	✓/CC	
2	142	3			s/BT		✓/CC				r/FR						✓/CC		o/FR	u/FR	✓/CC
3	501	5			r/FR		r/FR					–/FR				✓/FR			u/BT	✓/CC	✓/CC
4	365	4			s/BT		r/FR					✓/FR				✓/FR			u/BT	o/FR	✓/CC
5	325	4					u/FR					✓/FR				–/FR			u/BT	✓/CC	
6	129	3										–/FR						✓	u/BT	o/FR	✓/BT
7	498	5			s/BT		u/FR					–/FR		o/FR		–/FR	✓/FR		u/BT	✓/BT	
8	301	4					✓/FR					s/BT		o/FR			–/CC		BT	✓/BT	
9	379	4					✓/CC					r/FR		–/FR		–/FR			u/FR	✓/BT	
10	516	5	s/BT									–/FR		–/FR		–/FR			o/CC	✓/CC	
11	329	4			s/BT		✓/CC					–/FR		–/FR			✓/CC		u/BT	✓/FR	
12	145	3									r/FR	–/FR		–/FR			✓/BT		✓/CC	✓/CC	
13	371	4					✓/CC					r/FR		–/FR		–/FR	✓/BT		✓/BT	✓/CC	
14	298	4					✓/CC					r/FR				u/FR	✓/CC		✓/CC	✓/CC	
15	520	5	r/FR				✓/CC					r/FR				u/FR	u/CC		o/FR	✓/CC	
16	318	4			s/BT		✓/CC					r/FR				u/FR	u/CC		o/FR	✓/CC	
17	141	3									✓/CC							✓	✓/CC		
18	352	4					✓/UA					r/BT				u/FR	o/FR		u/FR	✓/CC	

Physical Aspects
✓ = on target
s = sliced
h = hooked
o = beyond target
u = short of target
r = right of target
l = left of target

Mental Aspects
NT = Negative Thinking
LA = Lack of Attentional Control
BT = Excess Body Tension
FR = Failure to use Routine
OA = Overaroused
UA = Underaroused
CC = Complete Mental Control

Summary:

Physical Aspects
✓ = 43   o = 9
s = 9   u = 14
h = 0   r = 0
         l = 11

Mental Aspects
NT = –   OA = –
LA = –   UA = 1
BT = 24 CC = 28
FR = 42

Note: From Golf: Better Practice for Better Play by L. Bunker & D. Owens, 1984, p. 210. Copyright 1984 by Leisure Press. Adapted by permission.

Figure 12.3 Sample Shotkeeper Scorecard.

FIGURE 12.4

KEYS TO SUCCESS

EFFECTIVE PRACTICE

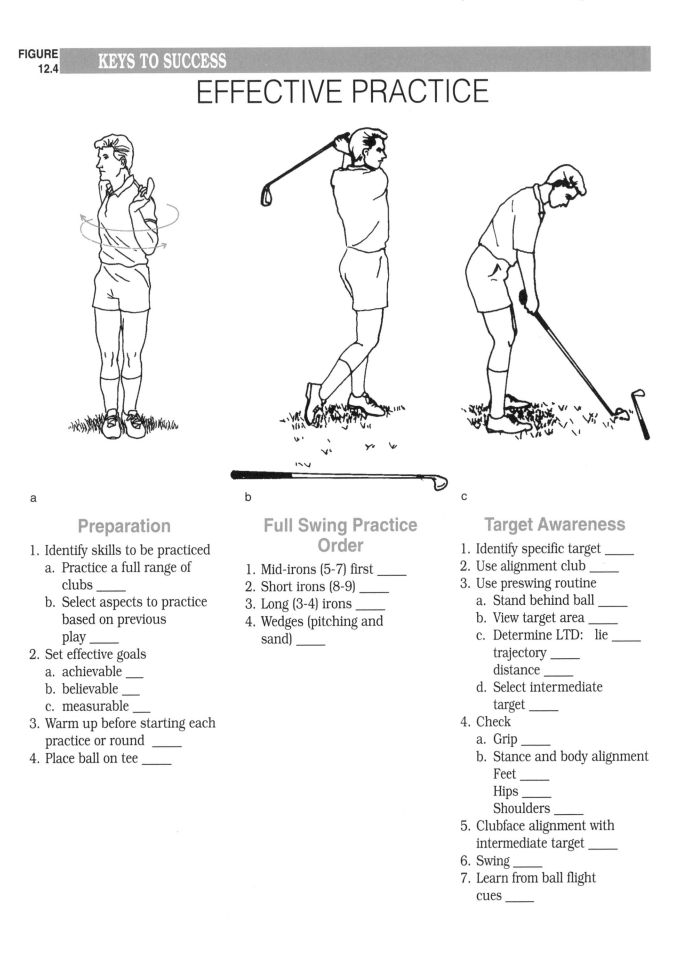

a   b   c

Preparation

1. Identify skills to be practiced
   a. Practice a full range of clubs ____
   b. Select aspects to practice based on previous play ____
2. Set effective goals
   a. achievable ___
   b. believable ___
   c. measurable ___
3. Warm up before starting each practice or round ____
4. Place ball on tee ____

Full Swing Practice Order

1. Mid-irons (5-7) first ____
2. Short irons (8-9) ____
3. Long (3-4) irons ____
4. Wedges (pitching and sand) ____

Target Awareness

1. Identify specific target ____
2. Use alignment club ____
3. Use preswing routine
   a. Stand behind ball ____
   b. View target area ____
   c. Determine LTD: lie ____
      trajectory ____
      distance ____
   d. Select intermediate target ____
4. Check
   a. Grip ____
   b. Stance and body alignment
      Feet ____
      Hips ____
      Shoulders ____
5. Clubface alignment with intermediate target ____
6. Swing ____
7. Learn from ball flight cues ____

If you notice that various shots travel straight but off-target, you may have an alignment problem or may be swinging the club in an unusual path. If the ball curves in flight, it may be due to the position of the clubface at impact, which varies because of the actions of the arms and hands. If the ball seems to fly too high or never gets off the ground, it may be due to the angle of approach (the downward swing of the club) or the point on the ball that the clubhead hits (below or above the center of the ball). These cues were discussed in Step 4 and can be reviewed during your practice.

There are also many specific drills that are great for practice. Review the drills presented in Steps 1 through 10. These are excellent practice exercises that allow you to feel comfortable with your swing and make it an "automatic" skill. Remember that the keys to developing a good golf swing are to be able to do the same thing each time and to sense what you did differently if the ball did not travel the way you intended.

When you decide to practice on your own, choose one or two aspects of your game to work on. Set specific goals for your practice and playing time. For example, if you are having difficulty getting enough distance from your shots, you may want to check to be sure that you have made enough pivot (Step 3) to allow a full and free swing. Exercises from previous steps such as the Wide-Whoosher Drill (Step 3) and the Body Rotation Drill (Step 1) would be very helpful. On the other hand, if you seem to lose your balance, try the One-Leg Toe Drill (Step 3) to learn to keep your swing centered, which aids your balance.

When you do a drill, it is important that you combine it with actual strokes. For example, practice the Cocking Drill Without a Ball (Step 3) 5 times. Then take 5 actual strokes. Then repeat the drill again, followed by 5 more actual strokes. Then repeat the drill twice, and hit 5 times, and, finally, just hit 10 balls in a row to finish the practice.

Why Set Practice Goals?

Once you have determined your strengths and weaknesses, you must convert these realizations into effective practice. In order to get the most out of practice, it is important to have predetermined objectives or goals. Goals help you maintain motivation, direct your attention, and help you know whether you are getting better. The best golfers know that they have the ability to be good, but also recognize that preparation is the key to success. Goal setting helps you focus your practice and capitalize on your skills. Steve Ballesteros, a great PGA tour player, once said, "The harder you prepare for anything, the higher your level of confidence about it, thus the less pressure you feel, thus the better you perform." It is a luscious cycle—prepare, practice, perform, build confidence!

The first phase of goal setting is to identify where you want to go. For example, if you wish to have a 15 handicap by the end of next summer, you must make a commitment to serious practice, focusing on your major weaknesses. In order to accomplish this, there are three steps to goal setting.

1. Use your identified strengths and weaknesses to establish goals.

2. State goals in specific and measurable terms.

3. Establish target dates and practice strategies.

Just wanting to get better is not enough. Nor is it appropriate to be all consumed by the idea of getting better and winning. Many professional golfers have emphasized how merely practicing more can get in your way—more is not always better. You must balance your love for the game and your ability to focus your attention on your practice. For example, both Tom Kite and Amy Alcott have described how they were practicing more than they needed to and thereby overtiring and making their games stale. They both discovered that it is best to practice *smarter*, not harder.

Goal setting and effective practice planning are the key to "smarter golf." Start by making a list of 4 or 5 long-term goals. For example, "I will improve my putting skills to average only 2.5 putts per hole." Your list of long-term goals focuses your attention, but it does not provide you with a detailed practice regimen. The next step is to make each of those goals more *specific* and *measurable*. By analyzing each long-term goal, you can establish specific short-term goals, such as the following:

■ Hit 8 of 10 putts to within 1 foot of these distances: 3, 4, 5, 6, 7, 8, 9 feet.

- Hit 7 of 10 5-irons 125 yards (plus or minus 10 yards).

- Hit 6 of 10 shots with a 5-wood straight.

- Hit 8 of 10 pitches within 15 yards of the target.

- Hit 7 of 10 chip shots with a 9-iron over my golf bag to within 3 feet of the hole from 10, 15, and 20 yards away.

Notice that some of the goals have higher expectations than others—6 of 10, as compared to 8 of 10—based on your particular skills. Each goal must be achievable within your own present skill level and the amount of time you want to practice.

It is also important to check that your goals are written in a positive, practice-directing fashion. State your goals in a way that focuses your attention on what you want to accomplish, not what you want to avoid. For example, you could have written a goal such as "Hook the ball not more than 3 of 10 times," but who knows—that might have caused you to slice it the rest of the time! Instead, you could state the goal as: "Hit a straight ball 7 of 10 times."

Each goal statement should identify achievable and measurable skills. It should also set the expectation that you accomplish these skills within a certain amount of time. Such *target dates* are not rigid deadlines, but they should be realistic lengths of time for you to attain your specific goals. Your target dates should help you focus your attention and be consistent in your practice by reminding you of the urgency of accomplishing your goals.

The third step in effective goal setting includes designing a practice strategy that helps you develop the skills necessary to meet your goals within the target date. Many of the practice techniques are easy to identify if you look back at the drills in each of the previous chapters. For example, practicing the Putting Ladder Drill or the Cluster Putting Drill (see Step 7) at least once per day for the next 10 days would be a good way to move toward accomplishing the first sample long-term goal listed previously.

EFFECTIVE PRACTICE AND GOAL SETTING

DRILLS

1. Identify Areas for Improvement Drill

To identify your areas for improvement, play 9 holes of golf and keep track of your shots with the Shotkeeper Scorecard (see Figure 12.2). Make a list of your physical and mental weaknesses: Look for any tendencies that repeat (e.g., 70% of shots go to the right of the target).

Success Goal = selecting one element for improvement in each of the following categories: Woods, long irons, mid-irons, short irons, chipping, pitching, putting, sand play, uneven lies, and mental control

Identify improvement needed:

Woods _____

Long irons _____

Mid-irons _____

Short irons _____

Chipping _____

Pitching _____

Putting _____

Sand play _____

Uneven lies _____

Mental control _____

✔ *Success Check*

- Identify goals in several areas ____
- Check each club ____
- Check each type of shot ____
- Consider both mental and physical aspects ____

2. Goal Setting Drill

To become a good practice golfer, you must be able to translate the weaknesses you have identified into specific goals, which then direct your practice. Assume that you discovered the following things from your Shotkeeper Scorecard:

a. 3 of 4 drives were sliced.

b. You failed routine 12 times.

c. 2 of 3 shots with 9-iron did not go high in the air.

d. 7 of 9 first putts were short of the hole.

State a goal for each observation. Be sure it is achievable, specific, measurable, and time-constrained.

◖ *Success Goal* = write and evaluate four well-stated goals with an achievable (A), specific (S), measurable (M), and time-constrained (T) goal statement for each of four areas needing improvement. Place a check under the column if it meets the criteria.

Improvement needed:

a. _____

b. _____

c. _____

d. _____

Goal statement: Check if it is:

	A	S	M	T
a. _____	—	—	—	—
b. _____	—	—	—	—
c. _____	—	—	—	—
d. _____	—	—	—	—

✔ *Success Check*

- Know yourself ____
- Goals are achievable (A), specific (S), measurable (M), and time-constrained (T) ____

3. Future Improvement Identification Drill

To plan your strategy for future improvement, identify your strengths and weaknesses systematically.

Success Goal = using the Shotkeeper Scorecard as a source of information to complete the future improvement targets card

Future Improvement Targets for Golf

Name _____   Date _____

For each of the clubs listed below, identify the typical characteristics you see in the ball flight coming from each kind of club. Use the same abbreviations used in the Shotkeeper Scorecard and describe each characteristic in terms of the number of times out of 10 that something happened (e.g., Driver: 7 of 10 slices).

Woods: Driver
 3- or 5-Wood
_____

Long Irons: 1-3
_____

Middle Irons: 4-6
_____

Short Irons: 7-9
_____

Pitching Wedge
_____

Sand Wedge
_____

Putter
_____

Success Check

• Goals should be A, S, M, T (achievable, specific, measurable, time-constrained) ____

4. Goal Achievement Card Drill

Using each of the characteristics identified as future improvement targets in Drill 1, write a specific goal statement for each element.

Each statement should be written as an achievable, specific, and measurable expectation with a specific target date.

Success Goal = identifying 5 specific goals and determining a practice strategy and target date for each

Goal Achievement Card

Name _____   Date _____

Skill	Specific Goal	Practice Strategy	Target Date
Example: Putting	Putt 7 of 10 into hole from 5 feet	Cluster Putting Drill 5 times; Ladder Drill 5 times; Line Drill 5 times	April 5

1. Long Irons or Woods

2. Middle Irons

3. Short Irons

4. Chipping and Pitching

5. Putting

✔ Success Check
• Goals should be achievable, specific, measurable ____
• Goals should have specific time lines ____

5. Consistency Improvement: Preshot Routines

It is very important that every shot in golf start from the same basic setup sequence (preshot routine). For this reason you may set a goal to use your preshot routine with at least 80% of your shots. In this drill, focus on the use of your routine, and the feel of the swing. Keep track of the number of times you are able to repeat exactly the same routine.

Success Goal = hitting 20 balls, using same setup routine each time ____

✔ Success Check
• Check LTD, connection with club (grip), alignment ____
• Assessing shot demands ____

1. (#) ____ determine lie of ball
2. (#) ____ determine desired trajectory
3. (#) ____ determine distance to target
4. (#) ____ select club to match the demands of the lie, trajectory, and distance (LTD)

• Standing behind ball

5. (#) ____ establish grip

6. (#) ____ select target landing area
7. (#) ____ select intermediate target

• Standing to side of ball

8. (#) ____ relocate intermediate target
9. (#) ____ align club with intermediate target
10. (#) ____ set feet
11. (#) ____ get comfortable
12. (#) ____ clear mind

To Increase Difficulty

- Vary target each time.
- Use a different club each time to increase the difficulty.

To Decrease Difficulty

- Use alignment clubs to help setup.
- Use markers (tees) to designate intermediate targets.

6. Varying the Target Drill

In golf, every shot aims at a different target. One goal or practice should be to work on target awareness and alignment. Start this drill by working with one club at a time (irons first, then woods). Select an iron of your choice. For example, take a 5-iron and use it to practice the full swing motion at one target, then vary the target location. Aim at a target that is to the left or right of your practice location, as well as one that is straight ahead.

Success Goal = 20 total swings toward targets with a full swing motion

5 swings straight ahead____
5 swings to target to left____
5 swings to target to right____
1 swing straight ahead____
1 swing to left____
1 swing to right____
1 swing to left____
1 swing straight ahead____

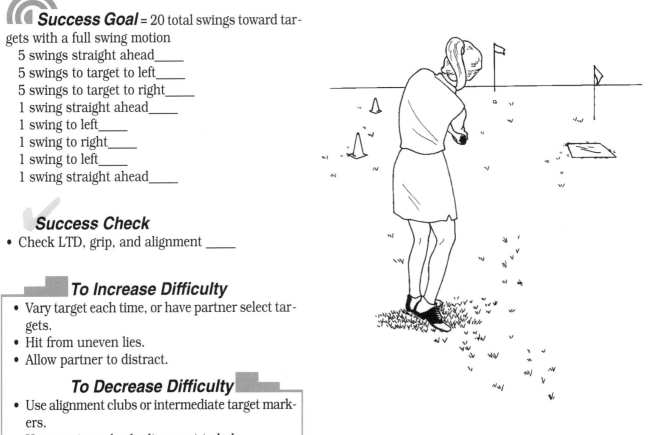

Success Check

- Check LTD, grip, and alignment ____

To Increase Difficulty

- Vary target each time, or have partner select targets.
- Hit from uneven lies.
- Allow partner to distract.

To Decrease Difficulty

- Use alignment clubs or intermediate target markers.
- Have partner check alignment to help.

7. Varying the Club Drill

One goal of practice should be to simulate actual playing conditions. For example, seldom do you hit the same club multiple times in a row. Similarly, you seldom get a perfect lie, so why not practice a variety of ball placements. Most practice areas have good lies when the ball sits on top of the grass and "bad" lies when the ball rests on bare ground or in a divot. When you hit a shot from these lies, notice the differences in how it feels when you strike the ball and how the ball flies after it is struck. Practice uneven lies whenever possible.

Success Goal = 25 total swings from good and poor lies

    5 swings from good lie____
    5 swings from bare spot____
    5 swings from good lie____
    5 swings from divot hole____
    5 swings from good lie____

To Increase Difficulty
- Vary shots hit from same spot.
- Add uphill/downhill and sidehill lies.

To Decrease Difficulty
- Use shallow divots and mild slopes.

Success Check
- Check lie ____
- Check stance ____
- Check alignment ____

8. Opposites Drill

It is important to be able to match the way extreme shots feel with what causes them to happen. To do this, identify pairs of opposite types of ball flight results: slices and hooks, topping the ball and hitting it "fat," and pushes and pulls.

Alternate hitting shots within each pair of opposites. For example, hit one slice and then one hook, or push one and then pull one shot. After hitting 3 sets of one pair of opposites, hit 6 good shots. Then go on to the next pair. Make each shot as different from its opposite as possible (e.g., a big hook and a big slice).

Success Goal = 36 total shots, hitting each pair 3 times (6 swings), with at least 4 of 6 attempts correct on each pair

    6 shots alternating slice and hook____
    6 good shots____
    6 shots alternating hitting on top of the ball and hitting fat____
    6 good shots____
    6 alternating push and pull____
    6 good shots____

To Increase Difficulty
- Have partner choose the type of shot.

To Decrease Difficulty
- Hit 2 or 3 shots alike and then switch to the opposite.

Success Check
- Focus on target, imagine sensory consequences ____
- Match real sensory consequences with anticipated feelings____

9. Pitch and Chip Drill

Most strokes in golf are saved around the green. Feeling comfortable with the short game in golf is critical to success. Practice acquiring a comfortable feel with both pitching (see Figure a) and chipping (see Figure b) by executing each shot 10 times, then alternating them to sense the different feelings.

Success Goal = 30 total shots using pitching or chipping

    10 shots with a pitching wedge or 9-iron at a pitching target 30-50 yards away____

    10 shots chipping with a 5- or 7-iron at a chipping target 10 yards away____

    3 shots pitching____

    3 shots chipping____

    2 shots pitching____

    2 shots chipping____

Success Check

• Check LTD to determine pitch vs. chip ____
• Check desired alignment ____
• Check posture ____

To Increase Difficulty

• Add obstacles to impede ball path or swing.
• Alternate pitch and chip shots.

a   Pitching

b   Chipping

10. Test Your Terminology

Understanding and using the proper terminology is important in communicating with other players and in enjoying the game of golf. Practice your terminology by naming and defining the parts of a golf hole and by identifying the terms for scoring. Check your answers with the preceding section and Figure 1 (on page 2).

Success Goal =

a. correctly label the parts of the golf hole diagrammed here

1. _____
2. _____
3. _____
4. _____
5. _____
6. _____
7. _____
8. _____

b. match the terms with their definitions

Term	Definition
birdie _____	1. a hole-in-one
bogey _____	2. two over par
ace _____	3. two under par
double bogey _____	4. one under par
eagle _____	5. one over par

Success Check

• Review *Rules of Golf* if unsure of terminology or rules ____

11. Practice at Scoring

All golfers should know the basic rules of golf. Each player is responsible for his or her own actions during play. The following situations requiring rulings are typical of those found on the course. Respond to each question; then check your answers by rereading the section on rules.

Success Goal = answer each of the following questions correctly

Lost Ball. You have hit your third shot into the woods and cannot find your ball.

a. Where do you play your next shot? _____

b. What is the penalty? _____

c. How many strokes will you have after you play your next ball? _____

Ball in a Hazard. You have hit your tee shot into a lateral water hazard.

a. What options do you have for playing your next shot? _____

b. What is the penalty? _____

c. How many strokes will you have after you play your next shot? _____

Out-of-Bounds. You have hit your fourth stroke out-of-bounds.

    a. Where do you play your next shot? _____

    b. What is the penalty? _____

    c. How many strokes will you have after you play your next shot? _____

Whiff. You have made 2 swing attempts to hit your tee shot. On the third attempt, you hit the ball about 50 yards into the fairway.

    a. Where do you play your next shot? _____

    b. What is the penalty? _____

    c. How many strokes will you have after you play your next shot? _____

Casual Water. You are playing after a heavy rainstorm, and your ball lands in a water puddle.

    a. Where do you play your next shot? _____

    b. What is the penalty? _____

    c. How many strokes will you have after you play your next shot? _____

12. Round of Golf Drill

Imagine each shot of a golf hole, picking out a target in your practice field for each one. Using your complete setup routine with each shot, hit the same sequence of real shots you would hit on the actual course. Never use the same two clubs in a row (unless you whiff one). Shift the target each time. This is the most realistic form of practice and should be done during each practice session. Practice like Nancy Lopez always practiced, by "actually visualizing the course conditions—where the pin is cut, where the bunkers are, how the match stands."

Imagine that you are playing a round of golf from the practice tee. Look out into the practice field and imagine an entire hole. The round starts on the first hole, perhaps a par 4. Start with a wood, or perhaps an iron if you are more comfortable with it. Actually hit the ball with that club. Follow this with a 5-iron on your second shot or, if you hit the first shot a long way, a 7- or 8-iron. Continue playing real shots until you have reached the green of the imaginary hole. Then take out a putter and stroke the ball toward the target you had chosen while on the practice tee. In your mind, see the ball go into the hole. Go on to the next imaginary tee.

Record the clubs used for each shot and the resultant ball flight. Also place an "R" near the club number if you used your routine.

Success Goal = playing 9 holes, selecting (and recording) a different shot and club each time, drawing shot diagrams for each "hole," and being sure to complete your entire preshot routine before each swing _____

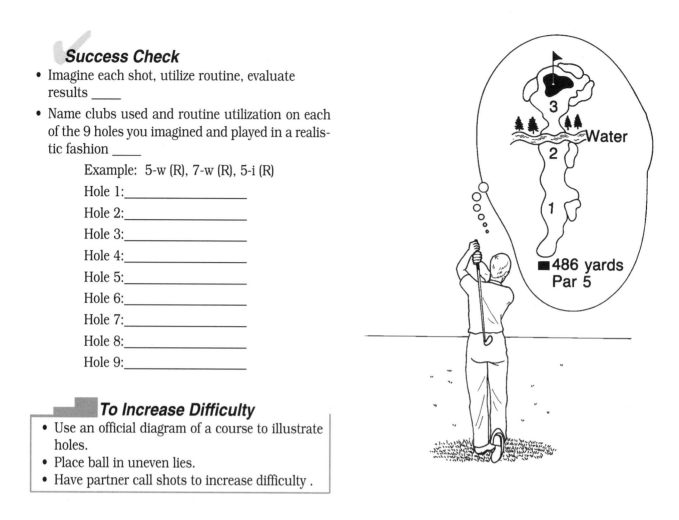

✔ Success Check

- Imagine each shot, utilize routine, evaluate results ____
- Name clubs used and routine utilization on each of the 9 holes you imagined and played in a realistic fashion ____

  Example: 5-w (R), 7-w (R), 5-i (R)

  Hole 1:_____

  Hole 2:_____

  Hole 3:_____

  Hole 4:_____

  Hole 5:_____

  Hole 6:_____

  Hole 7:_____

  Hole 8:_____

  Hole 9:_____

To Increase Difficulty

- Use an official diagram of a course to illustrate holes.
- Place ball in uneven lies.
- Have partner call shots to increase difficulty .

13. Shotkeeping Drill: Using Shotkeeper from Practice Tee

Using a Shotkeeper to record the results of each swing, play six holes of golf from the practice tee. For each hole, diagram and record the specific clubs used, the shot resulting from each swing, and the mental aspects present when you took the swing.

📶 Success Goal = pretend that you are playing 6 holes, diagram them (see example holes), record each club used and physical and mental aspects of shots, then tally summary results in terms of characteristics

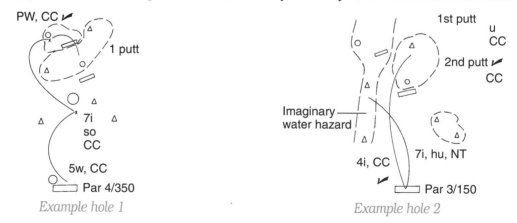

Example hole 1

Example hole 2

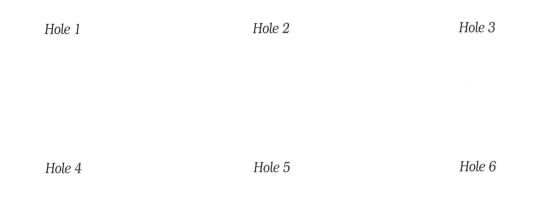

Hole 1   Hole 2   Hole 3

Hole 4   Hole 5   Hole 6

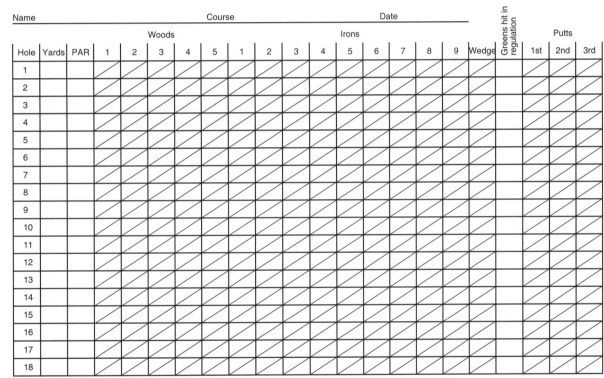

Performance Chart

Hole	Yards	PAR	Woods 1	2	3	4	5	Irons 1	2	3	4	5	6	7	8	9	Wedge	Greens hit in regulation	Putts 1st	2nd	3rd
1																					
2																					
3																					
4																					
5																					
6																					
7																					
8																					
9																					
10																					
11																					
12																					
13																					
14																					
15																					
16																					
17																					
18																					

Physical Aspects
✓ = on target
s = sliced
h = hooked
o = beyond target
u = short of target
r = right of target
l = left of target

Mental Aspects
NT = Negative Thinking
LA = Lack of Attentional Control
BT = Excess Body Tension
FR = Failure to use Routine
OA = Overaroused
UA = Underaroused
CC = Complete Mental Control

Summary:

Physical Aspects
✓ =   o =
s =   u =
h =   r =
        l =

Mental Aspects
NT =   OA =
LA =   UA =
BT =   CC =
FR =

Note: From *Golf: Better Practice for Better Play* by L. Bunker & D. Owens, 1984, p. 210. Copyright 1984 by Leisure Press. Adapted by permission.

✔ Success Check

• Record both physical and mental aspects of each shot ____

To Decrease Difficulty

• Record either physical or mental aspects (not both).

14. Plotting Hole

Play at least 6 holes of golf and plot your shots and mental states on a diagram of the holes on a Shotkeeper Scorecard (see Appendix). Summarize your performance by tallying the results for each club used and the types of physical and mental behaviors. For example, how many times did you hit the ball to the right or left? How many times did you fail to utilize your routine?

Success Goal = note at least one mental and one physical aspect for each shot ____
Fill in Shotkeeper Scorecard and summarize aspects noted ____

To Decrease Difficulty
• Record physical aspects only.
• Record psychological aspects only.

Success Check
• Record both physical and psychological aspects of each shot ____

EFFECTIVE PRACTICE SUCCESS SUMMARY

In evaluating the effectiveness of your practice, answer these three questions:

1. Did I identify the most important things to practice?
2. Did I set achievable, believable, and measurable goals to direct my practice?
3. Did I practice effectively?

Review the Keys to Success for Effective Practice identified in Figure 12.4 and place a check on the line for each element you consider when you plan your practice.

Using the Shotkeeper Scorecard you can identify your ball flight tendencies and the *most important* things to practice. Look for your overall tendencies, but be careful not to be too critical. Set both long- term and intermediate goals. Trust your strengths, but work on your weaknesses in order to be a great golfer. But be careful not to overanalyze; use your weaknessess to direct your practice. Remember, as Tom Kite said, "If you analyze every shot for mechanical flaws, sooner or later you're going to find some and it's going to be very difficult for you to trust."

RATING YOUR GOLF PROGRESS

There are general success goals in learning golf. One is to develop an appreciation for the game and a desire to pursue it as a leisure activity. The second goal is to achieve a level of skill that allows you to participate in and enjoy the game. The third is to have adequate knowledge of the skills of golf so that you can continue to learn and improve as you play the game.

Rate each of the following aspects of your learning experience. **4** = Strongly agree, **3** = Agree, **2** = Disagree, **1** = Strongly disagree

1. Overall I learned a great deal in using this book. _____
2. I improved my golf skills. _____
3. I enjoy playing golf. _____
4. I worked hard in following the drill format. _____
5. I would feel comfortable playing golf with my family and friends. _____
6. This book is a good resource for helping me learn and practice golf. _____

Physical Skills

The following is a list of the physical skills and on-course skills used in playing golf. During your practice sessions you may have practiced some or all of them. Now rate yourself on each of the skills you learned. **4** = Very successful, **3** = Fairly successful, **2** = Partially successful, **1** = Unsuccessful

Setup (consistency) _____

Grip _____

Alignment of body _____

Basic full swing motion

  With irons _____

  With woods _____

Pitching _____

Chipping _____

Putting _____

Sand

  Explosion shot _____

  Buried lie shot _____

Uneven lies

  Sidehill _____

  Uphill/downhill _____

Psychological and Mental Skills

Enjoying the game of golf and playing it successfully require several types of mental skills. You need to know the basic terms associated with golf and the rules of the game so that you can play fairly. You also need to know and demonstrate the etiquette of golf so that you and your playing partners can enjoy a safe and friendly experience. Also, you must be able to control your thoughts and emotions so that you can confidently and capably demonstrate the skills you practice. **4** = Understand and can use properly, **3** = Can define, **2** = Recognize but could not define, **1** = Unknown to me

Terminology

Parts of the golf course ____
Parts of the golf club ____
Terms related to scoring (e.g., birdie, bogey) ____

Rules and Penalties

Lost ball ____
Out-of-bounds ____
Water hazards ____
Hitting the flag ____

Etiquette

Order of play ____
Tending the flag ____
Playing through ____

Courtesy on the Course

Replace divots ____
Rake bunkers ____
Repair ball marks ____
Keep carts where they belong ____

Mental Skills

Use preshot routine ____
Use an intermediate target ____
Use alignment clubs to practice ____
Avoid negative thoughts and images ____
Identify the strengths and weaknesses of a hole in order to plan strategy ____

Now look back at this self-rating inventory. Reread each question and answer it carefully. What does it tell you about your golf skills, areas of strengths and weaknesses, and desire to play golf in the future?

It is important that you finish each practice session wanting to come back for another one. Some teachers suggest that for the last few shots of the day, you should focus on executing the most perfect swing possible. Once you have executed one of your best shots, stop. This allows you to walk away feeling good, remembering that great shot. Don't worry about hitting every single ball in your pile—it is better to have a great memory to store away, to savor the good feel of a good shot. Remember to replace the bad shots (by hitting or imagining good ones) and store the good shots in your memory for future reference—replay the good, replace the bad!

The most important thing about effective practice is that it must be purposeful and maintain your attention. As Jack Nicklaus said, "I learned a long time ago that there is a limit to the number of shots you can hit effectively before losing your concentration on your basic objectives."

APPENDIX: SHOTKEEPER SCORECARD

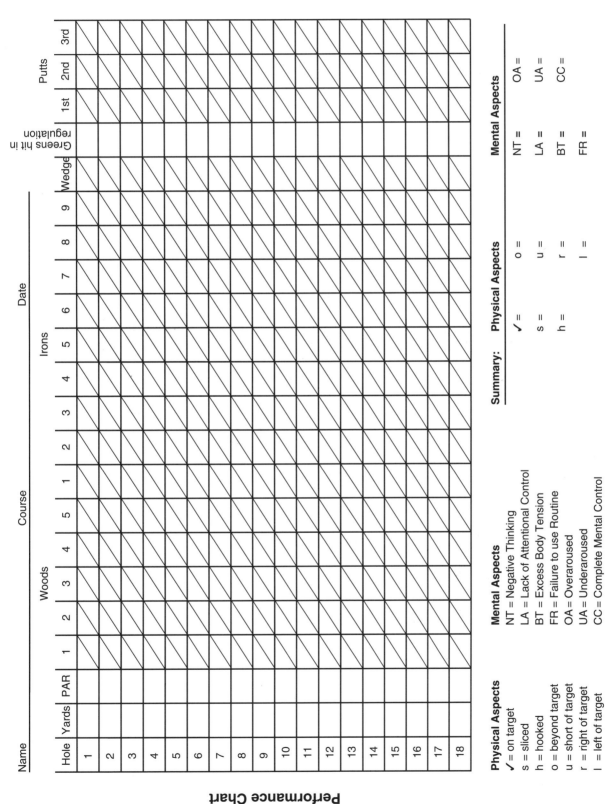

Performance Chart

Hole	Yards	PAR	Woods 1	2	3	4	5	1	2	3	4	Irons 5	6	7	8	9	Wedge	Greens hit in regulation	Putts 1st	2nd	3rd
1																					
2																					
3																					
4																					
5																					
6																					
7																					
8																					
9																					
10																					
11																					
12																					
13																					
14																					
15																					
16																					
17																					
18																					

Name _____

Course _____

Date _____

Physical Aspects

✓ = on target
s = sliced
h = hooked
o = beyond target
u = short of target
r = right of target
l = left of target

Mental Aspects

NT = Negative Thinking
LA = Lack of Attentional Control
BT = Excess Body Tension
FR = Failure to use Routine
OA = Overaroused
UA = Underaroused
CC = Complete Mental Control

Summary:

Physical Aspects

✓ =
s =
h =

o =
u =
r =
l =

Mental Aspects

NT =
LA =
BT =
FR =

OA =
UA =
CC =

Note: From *Golf: Better Practice for Better Play* by L. Bunker & D. Owens, 1984, p. 210. Copyright 1984 by Leisure Press. Adapted by permission.

ABOUT THE AUTHORS

DeDe Owens, EdD, is the Director of Golf Instruction at Cog Hill Golf Club in Lemont, Illinois, and a member of Wilson Sporting Goods Staff and Golf Digest Magazine Advisory Panel. A former professional on the Ladies Professional Golf Association tour, she holds the LPGA's Master Teacher ranking. She has been selected Midwest Teacher of the Year five times (1989-1993) and was the National LPGA Teacher of the year in 1978 and 1993. She was the National President of the LPGA Teaching Division from 1994-1996.

In 1986 Dr. Owens received the Joe Graffis Award from the National Golf Foundation for her "outstanding contribution to golf education." Her dedication to golf is obvious in everything she does. She is a full-time golf professional and consultant now, but she has also shared her skills as a faculty member at the University of North Carolina, Delta State University, Illinois State University, and the University of Virginia. Dr. Owens has written four other books, including *Golf for Special Populations*, *Golf: Better Practice for Better Play*, *Advanced Golf: Steps to Success*, and *Coaching Golf Effectively*, all published by Human Kinetics.

Linda K. Bunker, PhD, is a sport psychologist, professor of physical education, and Associate Dean for Academic and Student Affairs at the University of Virginia. She has been a consultant for both the National Golf Foundation and the Ladies Professional Golf Association, is a member of the National Youth Sport Coalition, and serves on the advisory boards of the Women's Sport Foundation and the Melpomene Institute, the Minneapolis-based research institute for women in sport.

Dr. Bunker has worked as a consultant to the Holland Golf Team and has provided golf workshops for PGA professionals from Japan, Holland, and the United States. She received the President's Award from the Women's Sports Foundation in 1994 and currently works with professionals in the ladies' and men's professional golf associations (LPGA and PGA). Widely published, she is the coauthor of many books, including *Mind Mastery for Winning Golf*; *Mind, Set and Match*; *Sport Psychology: Maximizing Sport Potential*; *Parenting Your Superstar*; *Golf: Better Practice for Better Play*; *Advanced Golf: Steps to Success*; and *Coaching Golf Effectively*.

*You'll find
other outstanding
golf resources at*

www.humankinetics.com

In the U.S. call

1-800-747-4457

Australia 08 8277 1555
Canada 1-800-465-7301
Europe .... +44 (0) 113 278 1708
New Zealand 09-309-1890

HUMAN KINETICS
The Premier Publisher for Sports & Fitness
P.O. Box 5076 • Champaign, IL 61825-5076 USA